Life in Hut Six

...scinated by the way Bletchley Park's commitment to absolute
...cy exercised such a powerful and enduring hold over those
...rked there – what a good thing that Mair Russell-Jones was
...ded to relax it a little, giving us this engaging account of life
...art of one of Britain's most important operations during the
Second World War. I greatly enjoyed this book."

EDWARD STOURTON, BROADCASTER AND AUTHOR

...ng story of a strong-minded and courageous Welsh woman's
...experiences at Bletchley Park. Not only does Mair Russell-
...describe what she actually did at Bletchley Park, but her
...is enlivened with a wealth of fascinating detail about working
...s, social life, ethos, and how being sworn to secrecy impacted
...and her relationships for many years to come. Once you pick
this book up, you won't want to put it down!"

OR ALLAN CHAPMAN, AUTHOR OF *SLAYING THE DRAGONS*

...ile. The memories kept secret so long before they could be told
emerge fresh and sharp."

ROFESSOR G. R. EVANS, UNIVERSITY OF CAMBRIDGE

...rom her home in the Welsh valleys, Mair Russell-Jones' quiet
...ic devotion to duty during the Second World War almost cost
...r life and reputation among unsympathetic family and friends.
... can't be easy telling your own parents' remarkable story but Gethin
succeeds without a trace of sentimentality. Humbling and inspiring."

STEVE GODDARD, CO-EDITOR, *SHIP OF FOOLS*

"Filled with emotion and intrigue, the secret life of one of Bletchley Park's code breakers has been told in such a captivating way to make this a fascinating true-life story. Indisputably the best title I've read for a very long time."

MARY HAMMOND, EDITOR, THE PLAIN TRUTH

"This is the story of an ordinary woman from the Welsh valleys made extraordinary by the exigencies of war. Mair Thomas would probably have been a Christian missionary had it not been for the Second World War. She was recruited for the intelligence team at Bletchley Park that cracked the Enigma code and made the Allied victory possible. Only after half a century did she tell the story of her secret life in Hut Six. Her story is told with the aid of her son, Gethin Russell-Jones. Other books have given dramatic, sometimes romanticised, accounts of the intelligence war. My Secret Life is remarkable for its unvarnished account of life at 'BP' – monotonous, wearying, unglamorous, and costly. Mair paid that cost till the end of her days. An absorbing read which gets closer to the humdrum reality of war."

DEREK WILSON, HISTORIAN AND AUTHOR

MAIR AND GETHIN RUSSELL-JONES

My Secret Life in Hut Six

One woman's experiences at Bletchley Park

LION

Published by Lion Books
an imprint of
Lion Hudson plc
Wilkinson House, Jordan Hill Road,
Oxford OX2 8DR, England
www.lionhudson.com/lion

ISBN 978 0 7459 5664 0
e-ISBN 978 0 7459 5665 7

First edition 2014

Some of the names in this book have been changed to
protect identities.

Acknowledgments
pp. 64-65: Extract from Winston Churchill's 4th June
1940 speech, copyright © Winston Churchill. Used by
permission of Curtis Brown.

Front cover image © Crown Copyright. By kind
permission of Director GCHQ.
Back cover image (Bletchley Park) © chrisdorney/
iStockphoto.

A catalogue record for this book is available from the
British Library

Printed and bound in the UK, July 2014, LH26

Contents

To Mair Eluned, in whom there was no shadow of guile

Author's Note

Throughout the rest of the book I have abbreviated Bletchley Park to BP. This has been done to reflect how my mother and other veterans affectionately refer to this nerve centre in the intelligence war.

Preface

This is the story of my mother's outrageous secret. Not a minor indiscretion or gross scandal; certainly not a chronicle of guilt. Thankfully my mother has never done guilt. This is an account of a confidence that she kept to herself for more than five decades, from the age of twenty-four until eighty-two. It is a ridiculous tale of silence, involving a young woman from the Welsh valleys and her role in dismantling the Third Reich.

It begins with two incidents. The first involves ill health; much of her life has been framed by often serious sickness. The second relates to my discovery of a book which features a photograph of her.

When, at the age of eighty-two, Mair chooses to break her silence and starts to reveal her secret past, she is mown down by a debilitating stroke after surgery on a hiatus hernia. She spends six months unconscious in an Intensive Care Unit. Her breathing is mechanically aided by means of a tube fed down her windpipe and into her lungs. Liquid food, high in protein, is pumped into her system at various points in the day.

It is clear, to the medical staff at least, that these are her final days and so the family drives and flies to the hospital from various points around the UK. This proves to be a false alarm and we return to our homes to wait for the alert. When finally we receive a phone call from the hospital informing us that she now has septicaemia, a grand, Latin-sounding word for blood poisoning, we of course understand that we are now in the end times of her life. The machine will be turned off with my father's consent and my mother and all her stories will die with her. Then comes the day when we are informed that she will almost certainly die. Once more the family gathers around the bedside, choking back the tears as our blind father quietly holds and strokes his wife's hand. She has not opened her eyes in months and there have been no responsive signs. However, on this day, when everything is at its darkest, she opens her eyes.

In order to prevent suffocation or infection, her tongue has been fastened outside her lips for most of the period in intensive care. But she is now looking at us; mute and vulnerable. Somehow her frail body, weakened by decades of sometimes serious ill health, has fought off the septicaemia. This is her D-Day.

She rallies, begins to recover, and after a few days the feeding pipe is removed. Still in a greatly weakened state, her breathing is laboured and a tracheostomy performed. This is an incision into her windpipe, which allows her to take in air more easily through an inserted tube. With the aid of this device she is able to breathe unaided. In the days, weeks, months and years that follow, my mother has to learn to speak again. Her powers of speech have been scrambled by the stroke, but it becomes evident that this will not be a permanent affliction. More serious is the damage to her larynx. These muscles had largely atrophied because of the tube in her oesophagus, and its lack of use for six months. For a long time, she can only manage words, names and very short sentences in a whisper. Then comes a squeak, followed by a weak tone.

Eventually she is moved to a small community hospital in Ystrad Mynach, a few miles north of Caerphilly where she lives with my father. This will be her home for another nine months, as she tries to reverse some of the physical losses she has suffered. She is never really able to walk after this episode. She is surrounded by aged patients, many suffering from dementia. Stable but by no means well, my eighty-something mother often opines: "They're very nice in here, but they're so old."

On an achingly beautiful Sunday afternoon in late summer, Clare, my wife, and I visit her and are given permission to push her in the wheelchair to the neighbouring park. A local brass band is playing, offering a benign and nostalgic soundtrack to children's play and young parents showing off their newborn babes. Other middle-aged children are also escorting their ancient parents; wheelchairs, pushchairs, mufflers, happy children and octogenarians are everywhere. The heat is gentle and the afternoon still luminous; one of those lazy, gracious days when everyone and everything feels connected and one.

After a while, we stop and listen to the music. My mother looks frail and small; crumpled into the wheelchair, tightly tucked in by layers of clothes. Despite the warmth she is wearing a coat, and further insulation is provided by a travel rug. A hat covers her head. She is still not well. Her throat is swathed in a white dressing, bearing a small dot of red, where the now removed tracheostomy tube is still oozing slightly. But the music is therapeutic and she is alive to it. Not that band music has ever been her thing; Bach, Mozart and Beethoven is the trinity she has always worshipped. But today she is captivated by the strains of wind and reed.

We buy some ice cream and she tries to munch and lick a choc ice. The band pipes up with a medley of Disney tunes, followed by famous film themes and then songs from the shows. Near the end of their set, they perform war tunes, material made famous by people such as Glenn Miller, Jimmy Dorsey, Vera Lynn and George Formby. This music was holding her, caressing her and giving her life. My eyes are already moistening with the grace of this occasion and the sense of goodwill in this park. We have been living with her last days for a long time.

I turn to her. She's trying to say something, but I can't hear over the sound of the band. I crane my neck and draw near to her face. I'm listening; she has my full attention. In a thin, small, squeaky whisper she says, "This music reminds me of the war. I feel I'm back in Bletchley Park." My mother has a story to tell.

The second incident is less dramatic but also part of the motivation to write a chronicle of my mother's wartime life and times. In 1998 my mother is given *The Secrets of Station X*, written by Michael Smith. I flick through the pages, curious but barely interested in its contents; my mother has yet to fully come out about her past in BP and I fail to make the connection between the book and her. Indeed, other BP titles have started appearing on her front room bookshelf but neither I nor my siblings make any comment. We have learned our lesson; best not to ask awkward questions about her wartime occupation. She has a litany which we have all memorized: "I worked for the Foreign Office in Bletchley Park."

Station X contains a number of photographs; machines, people and buildings. These grainy black and white images now grab my attention, opening my eyes to a place of which I know next to nothing. In particular my attention is drawn to one which bears the caption "Hut Six Decoding Room". Seven smartly dressed women, frozen in time, stare intently at machines that are on their desks. As I look at it closely I recognize the woman at the far end of the room, bathed in an eerie, beatific glow. Her posture and demeanour look very familiar. It reminds me of another picture taken a few years earlier, where my mother is playing the piano as a student. My parents keep all the family photos in an old and battered Huntley & Palmers biscuit tin, so I fish the picture out and compare it with the one in the book. It has to be her. I show it to her and she confirms her identity.

She even remembers the day it was taken.

We were busy at our work when one of the women who supervised the hut told us that a photographer had arrived at BP and would be coming to take photos. He was there to commemorate the opening of the new huts and we shouldn't be alarmed. The photographs would never be published, as that would be a serious breach of the Official Secrets Act. They would simply be seen by the prime minister and other very senior officials. She then left the machine room and we went back to our work.

It was always dark in BP. It didn't matter whether you were in the huts or the new blocks, the time of day or even season of the year. The electric lights were generally on, shedding a kind of spooky light. It always felt like night-time in there, no matter the season or time of day. The concentration you can see etched on our faces was typical of the working environment. It was intense. The daily riddles we faced produced a heavy and strange intensity; we were working on impossible codes and it was often deeply boring.

The image is inevitably silent and sanitized, rather like a scene from a suburban library in the war years. But there's one smell you need to imagine, while staring at this and all the other BP images.

The smell of nicotine was everywhere. Every shift had its fair share of smokers; women as well as men. I never smoked, but I was probably in the minority. And the more focused and intense the atmosphere, the greater was the stink of tobacco. There were some days when you felt there was a yellow mist hanging about the rooms. The ceilings in the original huts and the new blocks all looked stained and brown after only a short while. There was always someone striking a match and lighting up a cigarette or pipe. And even though I've never liked smoking, the smell of tobacco is quite comforting. Ever since my days in BP, the smell of a certain kind of tobacco, I couldn't tell you which, always takes me back to the manager's office in Hut Six.

As my mother recalls, the photograph is part of a sequence of shots taken in 1943 to commemorate the building of new blocks to accommodate the workforce that has outgrown the cramped huts. BP has grown from a few dozen workers in 1939 to more than 5,000.

That afternoon, after our supervisor returned to her office, we went on trying to make sense of endless flashing symbols. You pressed one key and another one would light up. That's when I became aware of another kind of flash. Out of the corner of my eye a sudden burst of white light caught my attention and at the far end I saw a man pointing a large camera at us all, along with a flash gun. He was a young man, somewhere in his thirties, sporting a pencil moustache, and he was smoking. He didn't introduce himself; he probably thought somebody else had done it for him. And he left without explanation. I'm not sure if anyone else turned towards him but if they did there was no discussion or recognition of this odd visit. We simply got back to what we were doing.

Gazing at the photo, my mother starts to explain what she was doing there. She tells me that this picture shows the machine room, where she worked on British copies of the machine used by the Germans to encrypt their messages. The German model was called the Enigma and it was fiendishly complicated; a mass of wheels, wires and keyboards.

It seemed to me that we were looking at wheels within wheels, for patterns and sequences without beginning or end.

She then compares her work at BP with an attempt to decipher some computer-generated drawings she was shown by one of my children.

A few years ago, one of my grandsons, Tom, showed me a book full of magic art. These were strange-looking paintings which apparently contained hidden pictures of animals. I couldn't see anything, but he saw elephants and bears and giraffes. He kept on telling me to relax my eyes, stare at the pictures, and I would see them too. But to no avail; it was so frustrating, but it also reminded me of the feelings I had in BP. Our job was to try to break those codes, and it was a most difficult task. In fact, during the years I worked there I never cracked a single code; if I did, no one ever told me.

This isn't strictly true. She was certainly part of a team that by 1944 was routinely breaking codes and passing on vital intelligence to Allied troops. But referring back to those days in BP, my mother consistently describes the lack of information given to employees. Not only do they not have the slightest idea what the other huts are doing, but they are not given any substantial feedback about their own progress. Occasionally there is a breakthrough in the hut, followed by cheering and clapping. But these incidents are few and far between. This reflects the extreme level of security in which they are working, but it also means that they labour under low morale. It will be decades before Mair realizes that she has been part of a team that changed the course and duration of the war. Former BP veteran and historian, Sir Harry Hinsley famously remarked that the code breakers of BP shortened the course of the war by at least two years. My mother will be well into her seventies before she understands this.

That picture is part of the genesis of this book and the beginning of my quest into my mother's secret past. Suppressing the human urge to spill the beans and tell her story has taken its toll on her. Decades of fear of state reprisal have robbed her of confidence. She carries the air of someone who is about to be found out, even though she knows she is free to talk.

This is my mother's memoir as related and understood by me, her youngest child.

The words in italic print are my mother Mair's first-hand account of being part of Britain's greatest wartime secret service: Bletchley Park. The rest is historical narrative, my reflections and those of others who knew my mother, either during her time at BP or later. Her mother tongue was Welsh, as was the case with many children growing up in Wales at the beginning of the twentieth century. It was the language of home and chapel. However, there are very few Welsh language words used in this book.

The four years I spent working there [at BP] were among my happiest, but I have spent most of my life trying to forget everything about it! I've given up on that now, enjoying the knowledge that I was part of one of the most exciting

teams that ever represented Britain. It was drummed into
us at the time that everything we did there was secret, and
when the war ended we were advised to forget everything.
So I deliberately tried to mentally burn all my memories of
that period. I blotted out feelings, events and people from
that time. But as others have told their stories of life in BP,
I realized that I could tell my own. And over the past few
years I have been piecing together the fragments of my life,
creating a tapestry of emotion and memory. Even though
over seventy years have now passed since I entered the gates
of the great manor house, that episode in my life seems
very real, as though it is still happening out there without
me being part of it. It's strange that even though so much
has happened to me since leaving BP, those four years have
probably influenced me more than the other ninety-two.

Chapter 1

January 1941 A Personal World War

As she recounted her story, my mother always returned to the day when her life changed for ever.

She was dead; I just knew it. I had a sickening hunch that something was dreadfully wrong and my friend had become a victim of the bombing of Cardiff. I can't explain why I had this sixth sense, but the smell of death was in the air that morning. The empty space next to me was filling with memories. Before the official announcement was made, grief was already numbing me. Poor Helen. I sat in the lecture theatre with my head reeling and thought about her short life, blown apart by a human-hating bomb.

That was the morning when it became my *war. Until then it was something that was happening over there, to somebody else. But that day it rudely interrupted my life and murdered my friend. I was now involved, whether I liked it or not.*

Helen's father was a university professor in the philosophy department. She was quiet, softly spoken and very good at

*languages, a dedicated student, tipped to get a First. We had
become good friends over the past year and I really liked
her company, although I can't say we were like sisters; some
people are part of your life without the relationship being
particularly deep. But on this day she was late arriving, which
was most unlike her. I tended to be the one always dashing to
get to lectures and generally arriving a few minutes late. In
fact, I had noticed there were a few absentees that morning.*

This is how 1941 begins for Mair. Back in Cardiff after a bleak
Christmas break, she is glad to be back in the city. Her mother's
death a few years earlier has left a chilly atmosphere at home as
family members struggle to come to terms with this untimely
loss. A pall of grief still hangs over her father, Dada, and Aunty
Lucy's backhanded comments are becoming ever more caustic.
In more normal times, the university term would start later in
the month, but the war is playing havoc with scholastic seasons.

Britain has suffered months of aerial attack during the Battle
of Britain, the German attempt to wipe out the RAF, and then the
beginning of the Blitz. It has been exposed to months of carefully
targeted bombardment. Dozens of cities have been bombed, tens
of thousands of people killed, and many fear that it's only a matter
of time before the nation will be under German occupation.

*This bombing campaign had been going on for months,
and we'd hoped that it would fizzle out before the New Year
began. But 1941 certainly started with a bang, even though
chapels and churches had been praying that this misery
would be over soon. The war was now into its second year:
we had been told it would be over within a few months.
I went back to Cardiff in time for the start of the new*

term. Everyone was on edge, constantly looking at the skies, expecting to see swarms of German aircraft. The train was crowded and any seasonal atmosphere had disappeared. You could sense an all-prevailing mixture of anger, distraction and determination. Air raid sirens were constantly going off, their wails adding to the prevailing mood of anxiety. The weather was bright and clear – just right for bombing, one of my friends said. Everyone in my hall of residence was nervous, even the girls who before Christmas were so blasé about war and saying they would drink their way through it all.

It all began on New Year's Day. By the time it was dark the tension was unbearable, tempered a little by the black humour and camaraderie of the other girls. At ten o'clock the bombs started falling… That's far too tame, makes it sound like snow or drizzle; these weapons of death were screaming and whining madly before that sickening thud and blast indicated they'd landed. I'd never heard anything like it before. I'd read about the London bombings only a few days before and seen some of the photographs, but somehow none of it seemed real. But this was frightening and we had no control over any of it.

I thought I was going to die or be horribly wounded. Along with a few others, we huddled in a little cwtch *[cupboard] in the basement of Aberdare Hall, the university's hall of residence for women. For some reason we didn't have an air raid shelter so the residents cramped together for safety and comfort in this little hideaway. It was terrifying, hearing the loud roar of the planes; it felt like they were just outside, scraping the tops of the buildings.*

The incendiary bombs were the worst and, curiously, the prettiest. For a brief few moments after they landed, everywhere was bathed in a magical blue light and there was no noise. Then came an explosion and a sudden eruption of flames. Death by burning. I think the incendiary device was followed by some kind of rocket that blew everything up. It was the kind of creative genius that was so pointless. Its only use was destruction and death. All that noise and colour meant that someone somewhere had been maimed, disfigured for life, or killed. I hoped Dada and my sister Beti were safe and unharmed.

The ten-hour air raid, during a full moon, begins in early evening, just after 6:35 p.m. Grangetown is the first area to be hit by a hundred German aircraft and bears the brunt of the attack, which continues for several hours before the planes head westwards. This isn't the first time that Cardiff is bombed, but it's one of the heaviest nights of fire in the capital city. A chapel in Llandaff Cathedral is also hit. The bakery owned by the Hollyman family on the corner of Stockland Street and Corporation Road is bombed and thirty-two people are killed, including at least five members of the Hollyman family. This large group is taking shelter in a nearby cellar when the bomb falls, leaving an 8 ft pile of rubble. In nearby Blackstone Street, seven relatives who have been to a funeral earlier in the day are also killed during the strike. Another fifty people lose their lives in Riverside's De Burgh Street. The toll is heavy. More than 427 people are seriously injured and nearly 350 homes are either destroyed or so severely damaged that they have to be demolished.

The planes then roar west, passing over Bridgend and the Garw Valley before discharging the rest of their load over Swansea. This town, over forty miles west of Cardiff, sees the most furious assaults, with much of the town centre turned into burning rubble.

As she walks to the lecture theatre the following morning, Mair sees the impact of the night terrors. There is debris everywhere.

*The air was smoky and acrid, you could taste it. I became
used to this taste during the war years. It was a vile
sensation of something poisonous and gritty at the back of
your throat and nose that you couldn't shift.*

In spite of the bombing, Cardiff is open for business. The university
welcomes students and staff to a new term; shopkeepers greet their
customers and the streets are full of pedestrians on their way to work.

*I made my way to the German department, unsure whether
I should be there or not. The city had been pummelled
during the night; the pounding and exploding had gone on
and on. The university itself was unharmed but some of
the buildings on Park Place looked as though they'd been
damaged. The atmosphere was eerily quiet; people were
getting on with their business, but in their own worlds.
Students, lecturers, other members of the public were locked
in their silence, processing the events of the past twelve
hours, wondering what the day might bring. We were
all living with shock and fear; dealing with the reality of
random and brutal destruction. Roads were closed to traffic.
Everyone was so down; you could almost taste the
depression. The lecture was half-hearted and pointless.
We were meant to be learning about the poetry of Goethe,
but the atmosphere was turgid and heavy. Everyone,
including the lecturer, was too distracted by the bombing to
concentrate. His words were drowned out by my frightened
thoughts; I could barely hear what he was saying, even
though he was only a few feet away.
Rumours were abounding about the number of students
killed in the strikes; especially the ones missing in the*

lecture theatre that morning. We gathered for comfort; the lecture was unimportant. It might as well have been about zoology for all the difference it made to us. We were all dazed; shaken by the horrid realization that this was our war. Until this point, most of my friends had associated this conflict with something happening "out there", but this changed everything. After half an hour, Helen still hadn't arrived and I longed for her to come into the room and make everything normal. I kept looking at the door, hoping that she would be the next person to come in.

Gossip and rumour abounded all day, worsening as every hour passed. But in the afternoon the dreadful news came through – Helen had died in the bombing. And not only Helen, but her entire family had been killed in the attack. They lived near the university; Column Road, I think. This bookish, quiet household was blown to eternity by a stray missile or maybe an incendiary device. This news shook me. It wasn't the first time I'd experienced the death of someone I knew, but this event fed the grief I still felt for Mama. The last time I saw Helen had been only a few weeks previously; just before Christmas. She was happy, looking forward to graduating, and thinking about taking a post-graduate degree in German, possibly at another university. And now she'd been killed by a German bomb. It was too vile for words.

This event still affects Mair, who is biting back tears as she tells the story. Even though it happened over seventy years ago, it's still fresh .enough to induce immediate grief. Her relationship with Helen barely went beyond the weekly routine of lectures, seminars and a few social visits, but the attachment is real enough to endure.

CHAPTER 2

1917–36 Rough Valley

The year 1917 is one of revolution, war, secrecy and bloody mindedness. It is also the year of Mair's birth. She is born on 17 October, a day which intersects with some of the year's most visceral events. On 15 October in Paris, dancer and socialite Mata Hari is shot by a French firing squad for spying for Germany. The evidence against her includes material gathered from a secret code breaking service run by British intelligence. The First World War is still raging, and on 17 October, pilots of the British Royal Flying Corps carry out their first bombing raid on German civilian targets, when two flights of de Havilland bombers attack the Burbach iron works and nearby railway lines near Saarbrücken. And on 25 October, exiled radical Vladimir Lenin takes over the leadership of the Bolshevik party, who then remove the provisional government from power and seize control of Russia. The ambitious Bolsheviks agree to a humiliating treaty with Germany, which enables the exhausted Russians to bow out of the war, by ceding vast tracts of land to the Germans. This in turn allows the German army to throw everything into its last attempt to win the war. They nearly succeed: but the following year, 1918, sees the final German capitulation. And in a quiet street in a distant Welsh valley, Mair Eluned Thomas is born. She is happily unaware that warfare with Germany and espionage will later dominate her life.

Her place of birth is 31 Albany Road, Pontycymer. This village lies at the head of the Garw Valley, one of the many in South Wales. *Garw* is a Welsh word meaning rough, even severe. Far from reflecting the cramped living conditions of its twentieth-century inhabitants, the word describes the rugged mountains and forests that dominate the valley. Unlike most of the other industrial valleys, it is more or less a cul-de-sac, except for a narrow lane which leads to the top of Blaengarw and on, treacherously, to the Rhondda and Afan valleys.

Like everywhere else in the region, coal is king; and its production employs thousands of men. It is a village, indeed a valley, of well-attended nonconformist Welsh and English-speaking chapels. It also boasts an abundance of burgeoning drinking houses with a different clientele. There are workmen's halls, libraries, literary and music societies and, of course, *eisteddfodau*. These cultural festivals, entirely in Welsh, demand the highest standards from all participants, even though many of them are still only young children. From their earliest years, Garw Valley children will become familiar with poetry, music, literature and performance. But this is no monoculture.

All kinds of people lived in Pontycymer. Work was scarce in those days and a lot of people came to work in the mines. They settled down and had their own families. I remember a great number of Irish people in the valley as well as Scots, and plenty from the north of England. I also had friends at school whose parents came from Somerset and Devon. And, of course, there were lots of Italians about the place. Most of the cafés were run by Italian families; I loved the gurgling, frothing sounds of those places and the steamy, cosy atmosphere you found inside. These families were well known and loved in the valley; they'd probably been there since the end of the last century. I was told that they were all from the same part of Italy, and had come to Wales in search of work at the time of a great depression in their homeland. They were amazingly enterprising, establishing cafés and fish and chips restaurants. One of the cafés in Pontycymer was Palledri's, and they sold the most amazing ice cream I'd ever tasted; deliciously sweet and creamy. At a time when there wasn't a lot of money about, the Italians somehow managed to make the most ordinary food taste exotic and different. Mama took me there once for cheese on toast and it was unlike anything we'd ever had at home.

The house of Mair's birth sits at the top of a steep hill, connected to a cluster of large semi-detached houses. Opposite are terraced cottages, built for socially mobile coal miners who have gained various promotions in the nearby pit. But the right-hand side of the street is populated by teachers, solicitors and doctors. (Local residents still refer to these dwellings today as the doctors' houses, even though that class moved to greener and more affluent pastures a long time ago.)

Mair is the first child to Thomas Thomas and Agnes Thomas. Agnes has three sisters: Ellen, Janet and Edith. Thomas is from a larger family. He has three brothers: Benjamin, David and Evan, and three sisters: Jane, Julia and Lucy. Both families are affluent by the standards of this overwhelmingly working-class area. Both sets of grandparents have died by the time Mair is born.

Thomas Thomas is a winding engineer in the nearby Ffaldau Colliery; a position of senior management and well paid. Agnes is a seamstress and has owned a ladies' fashion shop in Pontycymer, where she sold her own handmade dresses, produced on her sewing machine. In 1921, a second child is added to the Thomas family, Beti.

Mair's father has a sparkling literary lineage. Ann Thomas, a distant eighteenth-century ancestor was the subject of a well-known potboiler, *The Maid of Cefn Ydfa* and also a folk song which is still performed today, *Bugeilio'r Gwenyth Gwyn* (tending the white wheat).

The only child of William and Catherine Thomas, Ann was born in Cefn Ydfa farm near Llangynwyd. Her father died when she was young, leaving her the entire estate. Despite her mother's social climbing intentions, Ann fell in love with Wil Hopcyn, a labourer and bard. Their secret affair was discovered and the couple forbidden to meet again. Ann's mother arranged for her to be married to local solicitor Anthony Maddocks, and the wedding took place in 1725. Ann died, it is said, of a broken heart in 1727.

Wil Hopcyn was credited as the composer of the folk song from its earliest days. In 1847, author Thomas Morgan published a volume of short stories including *The Maid of Cefn Ydfa*.

Thomas Thomas owns two houses; the one in which the family lives, called Bryn Cerdd (hill of music) and a terraced cottage opposite. Throughout Mair's life, much mention is made of the house on the other side of the street. She is repeatedly told by her father that this will be her inheritance. But before his death in 1955, when suffering from the early stages of dementia, he tells Mair in great distress that a great injustice has occurred. In Welsh, he wails at her, "Mair, they've wronged you, they've wronged you." He claims that he has been forced to change the will and gift the house to others. When the will is finally read after his death, there has indeed been a late codicil. Mair inherits nothing.

The family's neighbours are all part of a small but affluent middle class. A few doors away lives Dr Dan Harry, who will later become headmaster of Garw Secondary School, the only grammar school in the valley. Even now Mair grimaces at the sound of his name, recalling a mean-spirited, self-interested individual. Next door were the Thomases, whose daughter Molly (born in 1932) would become notorious as the London artist and socialite Molly Parkin.

This literary lineage, and the tradition of land ownership in the family, means that Mair's upbringing is significantly different to the experience of most people living in the South Wales valleys at this time. To coin a Welsh word, she is a member of the *crachach* (posh class). Contemporary photographs of the valley show generations of its citizens in soot-soiled and threadbare garments; white skin permanently stained by coal dust and smoke. These are proud and poor people living in polluted times. Not so Mair: the pictures taken of her and Beti reveal clean linen, healthy skin and the sheen of privilege.

We had a maid called Rhilda. She cleaned the house and looked after Beti and me. She lived in one of the nearby streets. Most of the people who lived on our side of the street kept maids; they were all well-off families with fathers that earned good money. But we were surrounded by miners' families who earned a pittance for their hard work.

When women got married, they gave up their jobs and stayed at home, keeping house. By the time Mama and Dada got married they were both getting on; he was nearly forty and my mother was thirty. Mama had been running her own dressmaking shop in Oxford Street for more than ten years, making and selling her own designs. This was a really successful business, but she gave it all up when she got married. Although she didn't own a business any more, she used to teach girls and women how to sew and make their own clothes.

Even though Mama did all the cooking and baking, Rhilda was forever cleaning and tidying up. More often than not, Dada's clothes were coated in soot from the mines and she worked hard to keep the home warm and clean. There was always a smell of cooking and baking in the house; Mama was forever baking pies and roasting beef, lamb and pork.

We didn't play out on the street. It wasn't the done thing in our street or any of the others. I played with Beti most of the time, and the house was always full of visitors, especially Dada's loud sisters who came and stayed for hours several times a week.

At the age of five, Mair is enrolled at the nearby Ffaldau Primary School in the infants section. This is not a period she remembers with any fondness whatsoever.

I had a horrible head teacher, Miss Williams. She was always shouting and hitting us children. She was nasty to everyone and never ever smiled. They'd call it child abuse these days. I was a sickly child and missed a lot of school when I was little. I had flu, measles, mumps and chicken pox; there were only a few vaccinations available in those days so there were always children at home ill. Because I missed so much school, Mama taught me to read at home.

I remember once, when I actually went to Ffaldau, I felt so ill that I laid my head down on the desk. Miss Williams wasn't having any of it. She started hitting me, trying to get me to pay attention and stop being so lazy. I was only five! Somehow or another, my mother came into the school just after it happened. Someone must have gone to tell her, I suppose. She really laid into the horrid teacher in front of the whole class for treating me so badly.

When I moved up to juniors, everything changed for the better. Miss Thomas was the head and she was a family friend. She was strict but fair, and liked children in a way that Miss Williams didn't. For some reason all the children referred to her as Fanny Bloomers; I can't remember why. She was a vivid character, loud and commanding but also fair. She also rode an enormous motorbike with gleaming metal handlebars, complete with goggles that eclipsed most of her face. She was always noticed, and her arrival anywhere was preceded by the violent growling and spluttering of her machine that had been built, so she said, during the First World War.

All the female teachers were called Miss, presumably because they were all unmarried. Mind you, lots of Garw Valley men had not returned from the war, so there were many widows around, and there were far more single women than eligible men. Dada had tried to enlist in the army; he felt very strongly about fighting for king and country, but he was told that his work in the mines was too important and he had to stay.

Mair's musical abilities are spotted and encouraged at a young age. Her parents are members of local choirs and keen to instil a love of music in their daughters. When she is five years old, Mair starts piano lessons with another Miss Thomas in Pontycymer.

She was very nice and she eventually married a Methodist minister. But after a few years she told my mother that she couldn't keep up with me and I needed a better teacher. Then Mama and Dada took me to Bridgend on the bus every week, to the Beethoven School of Music. My teacher was Miss Howells and I stayed with her until I went up to Grade Eight when I was fifteen.

In 1926 the effects of General Strike and its repercussions are being felt in the Garw Valley. Even though it only lasts for ten days in May, the miners stay out until the end of the year. Some are sacked and replaced by men from Somerset and the north of England. Social tensions rise and the police are called to intervene on a few occasions. Nine-year-old Mair observes the fallout of the increasing poverty in the valley.

I went to the shops with Mama and I saw this long queue of people stretching from the church right down Oxford Street. Some of the people I recognized, and there were quite a few from my school in the crowd. I asked Mama what they were doing and she said there was a soup kitchen in the church, feeding people who couldn't afford to buy food. She said most of the valley men had lost their jobs and this was the only way they could eat. I asked her if we were going to the soup kitchen, but she said that Dada had a good, safe, job and we wouldn't need to.

Even in our small valley, I noticed lots of new faces and families. They came from all over the country and were

looking for work, even though it was in short supply. These
were desperate times. A number of them were clearly very
poor and wore very tattered clothing. Quite a few of the
children I saw had no shoes on.

I heard of a church minister by the name of Revd D.
S. Jones; he had such compassion for these wandering
itinerants that he provided breakfast for them every day in
his church. His members were so affronted by this that they
told him to stop as they didn't want those kind of people
coming into their church. He refused and carried on feeding
them. The poor man was then sacked by his congregation.

Mair's talent for playing the piano is rewarded by a rapid succession
through various exams. By the time she passes her scholarship
exam to the local grammar school, she has completed Grade
Four and will soon be successful in Grade Five. She nurtures an
ambition to become a concert pianist, a dream that is encouraged
by parents and teachers alike. She is compliant, bright, ambitious
and eager to shine. Mair's love of piano playing spills over into
later life. My memories of returning home from school cannot
be separated from the sound of piano lessons booming through
every room. My mother never lifts her voice or loses her temper,
even though she is teaching children who are murdering the
scales and butchering the works of the great composers.

As soon as Mair enters Garw Secondary School at the age of
eleven, she becomes the school pianist; a position she occupies
until she leaves at the age of eighteen.

My cousin Eb, Aunty Caroline's son (she was known as
Aunty Car), was the history master at the school, and he
knew I could play the piano well. He recommended me to

the headmaster and I was appointed as the school pianist.
I played every morning in school assembly and other
important school functions.

Mair is entered for various local and national *eisteddfodau* and
these provided a wider platform for this fiercely ambitious and
competitive young pianist. Diligent in her studies, she works
hard and particularly enjoys Welsh, English, Latin and science.
Her competitive spirit and drive surface in PE. Even though no
one else in the family has demonstrated sporting prowess, Mair
shines on the tennis court.

I loved playing and took to it more than any of the other
games we had to play. I even became the school tennis
champion in form five. I was the only girl who played tennis
and I beat a boy, Mervyn Bridgeways, in order to win the
cup. I felt so proud, but it was a little embarrassing for
Mervyn as he lived in the same street as we did, but on the
opposite side of the road.

As Mair prepares for that summer's matriculation, her mother
receives devastating news. Agnes has been unwell for some weeks,
complaining of tiredness and general pain. Her appetite has gone
and she looks pale, her lips sporting a bluish hue. After several
visits from the family's GP and several blood tests, a diagnosis is
obtained: pernicious anaemia. She is now terminally ill; there is
no remedy for this condition. It can only result in death.

When Mama wasn't well I went to see Aunty Nellie (Ellen)
when I was studying and revising; the atmosphere at home
was so heavy and sad. One day, Dada sat us down and told

*Beti and me that Mama was dying and that we must pray
for her and be as brave as we could. She took to her bed for
six months and only very rarely was she able to get up. She
changed from being a quiet and strong mother to a frail
little thing in only a few weeks. It was horrible.*

As she waits for the results of her matriculation exams in 1934,
Mair is invited by some close family friends to join them on their
farm near Aberystwyth. The Morgans have four daughters and
Mair is friendly with the two older girls, Delyth and Tydfil. The
family worship in a Welsh-speaking church on Sunday mornings
and in the evening they attend an English-speaking church. On
the Sunday that Mair is with them, a Scottish minister named
George Patterson is preaching.

*I felt he was speaking to me personally, even though the
church was full that night. I'd never heard anything like
this before. Back home in Pontycymer I was used to going
to Bethel, a Calvinistic Methodist church but this was so
different. He spoke about faith as a personal relationship
with God and everything in me said yes, I want that! I
went up to Mr Patterson after the service and told him
I wanted to become a Christian. He was very kind and
prayed with me.*

*When I arrived home after the holiday, I told Mama
and Dada about my decision and they were really pleased.
Even Beti said she wanted to become a Christian. My
mother's sisters were not so enthusiastic. They thought it
was all a bit too emotional and I would get over it quickly
enough.*

Faith, resilience and a fighting spirit have been Mair's main traits ever since this period. Despite her father's acceptance of this new faith experience, other close relatives are less impressed. She is told to be wary of emotional Christianity and not to turn her back on the religion she has known all her life and which has served her family well. This only stiffens her resolve to be different to the others.

By the time Mair returns home from Aberystwyth, Mama has become gravely ill and is fighting for her life.

The last part of 1934 and beginning of 1935 were horrid. Mama got weaker and weaker and a dreadful heaviness hung over our house. Poor little Beti was particularly traumatized by it all. One of Dada's sisters, Aunty Jane, came to stay with us and she was lovely with Beti and me. On Christmas Day, Dada carried Mama down to have dinner with us but she was gaunt and weak and couldn't eat anything. She was like a tiny, frail bird and it was heartbreaking to see the rampaging power of this incurable disease. I could tell it would only be a matter of time before she died. She wasn't really with us by then, as though she was already passing over.

Agnes dies in February 1935, age forty-seven. Mair has turned seventeen and Beti is thirteen.

Poor little Beti was so upset and sad without Mama; we all were. Dada grieved and mourned for a long time.

The weather that month is bitterly cold and bright; conditions that persist until the day of the funeral. Following traditional

Welsh custom, Agnes's body has been laid out in the parlour of 31 Albany Road between death and the funeral. Family, neighbours and friends came to pay their respects and the aunties took over, taking care of the endless cups of tea and sandwiches. The funeral also follows time-honoured custom and is centred on the home.

Dada bought me a new grey frock, navy shoes and a new hat for the funeral. Beti was too young to come; she was looked after by other relatives. The minister from Bethel took the service in our home and the house was packed with mourners. We then had a service outside the house and the whole street came out of their homes and took part... The day had a dreamy, unreal feel. I held Dada's hand for most of it but I couldn't bring myself to look at him; I knew that if I caught his eye I would not be able to stop crying. After the service outside we followed the coffin down the hill, along Alexandra Road until we got to the cemetery. It felt like the whole village was with us; it felt so comforting, like an enormous blanket was comforting us all.

As the year progresses, Thomas, Mair and Beti try to adapt to life without Agnes. Aunty Jane's presence is now a daily fixture; arriving early in the morning and leaving for her own home later in the day. She cooks all the meals and forms a powerful bond with Beti. Thomas keeps his normal work routines and barely takes any compassionate leave. But the atmosphere at home is thin, empty and lifeless.

A disturbing episode illustrates the growing tensions between Mair and the aunts on her father's side of the family. One day she is challenged that she is not displaying enough grief over her mother's death.

I was very aware of controlling my feelings at that age; I always have been like that. I missed my mother dreadfully, but I didn't show these feelings; I preferred to cry in my own bedroom. But one day, I was alone in the house with two of my aunties and they started on me. They told me it was unnatural that I wasn't grieving properly: didn't I realize how much my mother loved me? My cool manner was dishonouring her memory. They kept on and on at me in this vein for the best part of an hour. They told me that they were going to make me cry and let the feelings come out. They succeeded all right. I started howling and shouting uncontrollably; I was hysterical. I'm not sure it was grief, rather the ghastly pressure I had been placed under. Dada arrived home and saw me slumped on the floor sobbing and wailing and he took me to my bedroom. I was ill for days afterwards; the doctor was called out and he gave me some medicine to help me sleep.

As a result of her conversion in the summer of 1934, Mair forges new friendships. George Patterson puts her in contact with a group of young people in Cardiff who meet every Saturday night in the city. They gather in the manse of the minister of the Heath Presbyterian Church, Mr Owen. She is now old enough to travel by train on her own and every Saturday evening she takes a bus to Bridgend and then a train to Cardiff. During these meetings she hears about a missionary training college called Mount Hermon in Streatham, south London.

I heard about Mount Hermon and I immediately felt drawn to that way of life. It had been a taxing year and I hadn't had much time to think about my faith or where I was going in my life. Becoming a concert pianist had lost its appeal after Mama's death and I couldn't see a future in Pontycymer. Dada was preoccupied with work and chapel and I hardly saw Beti; she was spending most of her spare time with the aunties and their children. My conversion experience was profound and I knew that nothing would be the same again, so towards the end of 1935 I applied to Mount Hermon college.

Her father is supportive of Mair's decision, but the other members of this close family have mixed feelings. A minority agree that this bright young woman needs to flee the nest and get on with her life. This is not the position taken by the majority of the interested parties; most of the formidable aunties are of the view that Mair's place is at home with her father and little sister. Only she can fill the void left by Agnes's death, and leaving home for study in general and missionary training in particular should not even be an option. But these feelings were toned down, largely out of respect for Dada.

Mair is aware that her decision is causing conflict, but she is determined to pursue her studies in London. Her application is successful and she is offered a place in the college. She completes her higher examinations in June 1936 and prepares for her new life in London.

I loved my family and my home, but I had this yearning for adventure. Quite a few of my aunts and cousins wanted me to stay and look after Dada and Beti, but I knew that my future lay elsewhere. Strange, really, I hardly knew anyone who'd moved away from Pontycymer; most people stayed and had families of their own. Each year a few pupils went off to university but no one I was close to. I found Pontycymer and the valley suffocating and I felt guilty for thinking like that. But since becoming a Christian I felt alive and excited. The world was opening up to me and I wanted to bite everything to the core. The words of a hymn by James Mountain that first I'd sung up in Aberystwyth were with me all the time.

Heav'n above is softer blue, Earth around is
    sweeter green!
Something lives in every hue Christless eyes have
    never seen;
Birds with gladder songs o'erflow, flowers with deeper
    beauties shine,
Since I know, as now I know, I am His, and He is mine.
Since I know, as now I know, I am His, and He is mine.

Those words expressed how I felt. I wanted more than I had and I was greedy for the future.

Over seventy years later, these are still her words. This is her rule of life. Now confined to a small room, her vision remains expansive. Education lifts you up, faith opens your eyes and music is the language of love.

CHAPTER 3

1936–38 London on the Eve of War

Mount Hermon Missionary Training College is an inter-denominational training college located at the far end of Streatham Common, in an area known as the Rookery. Established in 1911, it is part of a growing network of training institutions with an emphasis on providing practical theological education, especially for women. Formal ordination is still largely a male-only pursuit; some denominations have a few female ministers, but this is not the case with either the Church in Wales or the Church of England. These new colleges are responding to the needs of overseas Christianity where there is greater flexibility on the issue of gender and leadership. Mount Hermon is exclusively for women, and the principal, Irene Crocker, presides over a largely female teaching faculty. The only exceptions are occasional visits by local male clergy.

Miss Crocker was very bright and persuasive. She was a classics scholar, and during chapel she would often read the Bible from the Hebrew or Greek before translating it to us.

*I wouldn't say she was particularly pretty; in fact, she was
rather plain. She had been a missionary; in the Belgian
Congo, I think. She was firm, austere and wouldn't stand for
any nonsense. But she was a very good and clear teacher.
And she was always fair in her dealings with people.
She genuinely believed that the day would come when
women would be ordained as clergy in the mainstream
denominations. I don't think any of us really believed her at
the time. It was possible even then for women to be ministers
in some denominations, but they were generally regarded as
poor cousins to the men. Miss Crocker would have none of
it, and she said that the mission field had opened her eyes to
the appalling needs of the world and the utter irrelevance of
gender issues. This was not a viewpoint that was shared by
many church leaders at the time. Of course they were men,
so they would say that, wouldn't they?*

Dada, Beti and Aunty Ellen travel to London with Mair. This is the family's first time in London and they are mesmerized by the size and busyness of the capital. Another train journey to Streatham and the day is spent walking around the college and enjoying the common and its rookery. Their parting is emotional with the realization that the family unit is once again being dismantled. But the rigorous lifestyle demanded by the near convent-like atmosphere of Mount Hermon leaves Mair little time for regret or reflection.

Chapel is held twice a day and attendance is compulsory. On Sundays the students are obliged to lead church services across south London in addition to their chapel duties. The tone of the college is a mixture of genteel revivalism, strict Bible teaching and an ethos of public service.

For the first time in my life I was in an environment where women were on an equal footing with men. I felt I didn't need to apologize for not being a man, and the freedom to learn and lead was so liberating. It was here that I really understood that Christians have a duty to serve their neighbours; not only through spreading the message, but through trying to make the lives of ordinary people a little happier and better.

The dress code was strict. We all had to wear a blue uniform. A navy dress with a white collar; navy jacket and navy bonnets. There was a lot of navy! We would often have to lead open-air meetings in busy streets, and people always came up mistaking us for the Salvation Army.

Each day was mapped out for us. We rose early at 6:30 and performed our household chores. This was followed by breakfast and college prayers in the chapel. Lectures began at nine and continued until 12:30. After lunch, our afternoons were spent in the community.

It doesn't take long for Mair's musicality to surface in the college, and within a matter of weeks she is made the college pianist. Although far removed from Garw Secondary School, she is adapting to her new life in this institution. At college services and civic functions, her piano accompaniment becomes a familiar feature of Mount Hermon life.

Along with two other students, Mair is assigned to work with a Jewish community, mostly children, in the East End. During the 1930s, London's East End witnesses a rapid influx of Jewish immigrants, many of them fleeing growing anti-Jewish persecution in mainland Europe, especially Germany. The Nuremberg Laws are passed in 1935, stripping the German Jews of many of their rights, and further amendments are made in the following years. Anti-Semitism is now enshrined in law. Jews are denied German citizenship, and marriage between Jews and non-Jews is forbidden.

After only a few weeks in her new home, Mair hears of a frightening anti-Semitic clash in an area just east of central London. On Sunday 4 October, just after tea, a group of students return unexpectedly from an open-air meeting in the Shadwell area of the East End.

They had gone to conduct an open-air just off Cable Street, somewhere between the city of London and Limehouse. I didn't know my way around London at that time, but I'd been told it was in the East End. The area was full of Jewish and Irish people and it was always busy and vibrant.

Open-air meetings were a feature of Mount Hermon. They happened about twice a week; everyone had to take part in them at some point. That's where we learned to speak in public, deal with hecklers and engage with people in matters of faith and belief.

When they came through the front door into the main hall, the students looked shaken up and drained of colour. Some of the girls were crying, and three or four of them had cuts to their faces. It seems that as they were setting up for the meeting, they became aware of loud chanting and shouting coming from Cable Street, just at the top of the road where they were. They could tell something was going badly wrong and a few of them ran to see what was going on.

They saw hundreds, if not thousands, of men in brown shirts marching and taunting the bystanders. They were saying things like "Jews go home" and "We don't want the

44

*Irish over here". But there was another equally large group
of men also marching in opposition to them and the police
were in the middle of it all. It was very frightening.*

*The streets around there are narrow; people and traffic
funnelled either into the city or further east. This small
group of students found themselves swallowed up into this
swirling tide of protest and were soon being pushed and
pulled by the angry crowd. One of the girls in that group
was numb with it all and said she'd seen unimaginable
anger and aggression. Gangs of men could be seen
punching, kicking and stabbing innocent bystanders. She
had watched an old man pushed over and kicked repeatedly
by four young men in brown shirts.*

*There were lots of police there, but the girls said that
they didn't intervene early enough and that by the time
they acted most of the damage had been done. Mounted
police rode into the crowds trying to disperse the marchers
and at one point a car was seen driving right at the crowd,
although it seems the march by the brown shirts was
abandoned. There were injured, bloody bodies everywhere
and most of the shops and businesses had broken windows
and doors. Somehow the girls managed to stay together and
made their escape back to the open-air team after about an
hour of their dreadful ordeal.*

*It was then that the bell rang and we were summoned to
evening chapel. There was a sombre mood over everyone,
and Miss Crocker addressed us. She looked very solemn
and her voice was shaking. She explained to us that she
had just spoken to the police in order to find out what had
happened. It transpired that the open-air team had been
caught up in a clash between a fascist organization and East*

45

*End protest groups. It was probably the worst incident of
civil disturbance in London for a hundred years. She said
that fascists hated the Jews and wanted to drive them out of
Europe. At that point her voice broke and she began to sob.
None of us knew what to do; she was normally such a strong
person. She gathered herself up after a minute or two and
said that this violence would not stop us sharing the love of
Christ in the East End, and we had to endeavour to stand
alongside our Jewish brothers and sisters.*

The incident in Cable Street had been initiated by Oswald Mosley
and his British Union of Fascists. This ideology has gained
support across Europe, and Adolf Hitler's National Socialist
(Nazi) Party is now in power in Germany. As part of his strategy
for a Greater Germany, his forces have occupied the Rhineland.
Benito Mussolini in Italy has his eyes on the creation of a new
Roman Empire under a fascist government. World war is still
three years away but the wind of expansionist dictatorship is
blowing. This incident awakens Mair to the vulnerability of the
Jewish people to fascist attack. It is the beginning of a lifetime's
respect and concern for their welfare.

Despite this unpromising introduction, the East End is a
revelation to Mair.

*I'd seen poverty before back home, but not like this. Rows
of streets with tiny terraced houses jammed up against
each other, and children everywhere. I'd hardly seen any
non-white faces in my life and here there were so many
nationalities rubbing shoulders with each other. There was
no aggravation or bother but the noise of shouting, playing
and laughter was deafening. But I knew I was among poor*

people. Children playing barefoot were common and they were often unkempt and ragged. And many of the houses held more than one family. I came across one street in Shoreditch where there were three Jewish families living in a two up two down terraced house. Having said that the people were very friendly to us and we were always being offered tea to drink. In many ways I felt really at home in the East End; the close-knit communities with people looking out for each other reminded me of life back in the valley.

Mair's remembrance of this contact with the Jews of the East End is laced with pain. Looking back through the lens of the holocaust, she feels a sense of frustration and guilt that neither she nor indeed anyone else knew about the events unfolding in Nazi Germany.

At the time I didn't think about why they were in this country. The children, like children everywhere, were lively and trusting and we were so busy teaching them. Sometimes their parents would come over and talk to me and I found out that many of these families came from affluent backgrounds. Quite a few of the children's fathers had been doctors, solicitors and bankers but were now living in very impoverished circumstances. I don't like using the word, but they had come over here looking for a better life and were living in slums that no one else would have lived in.

But it isn't all 'Onward, Christian Soldiers' and moral zeal for the ladies in Mount Hermon. On Saturday afternoons, the young acolytes are allowed to shed their bonnets and navy clothing and wear what Mair called mufti. This clothing is not dramatically different to the style worn by the students each day, except that bonnets do not feature. For an afternoon once a week they are able to fill their time as they wish. Some visit the shops and tea houses of Streatham, but Mair's inevitable competitiveness comes to the fore.

I acquired a liking for croquet – not a game I'd played before and it was unknown in Pontycymer. The most satisfying aspect, of course, is being able to knock the other person's ball out of the way in order to get your own through the hoops. It was a very competitive atmosphere and I used to look forward to this treat at the end of the week. We had all been so good and dutiful all week and this was our one chance of letting our hair down. However, we were only able to play during spring, summer and autumn as the college lawn and grounds were almost sacrosanct. But the grounds were so beautiful and the summers of 1936 and 37 were long and warm.

The year 1936 ends on a note of high drama. The abdication of King Edward VIII is suddenly announced on 11 December and the throne now passes to his younger brother, Albert who assumes the regal name of King George V1. There is no King's speech on Christmas Day.

It all came as a huge shock, although it wasn't long before the press started running reports about his affair with Wallis Simpson. The country seemed to be on the up at the time and this came as a great blow to everyone.

By now Mair has settled into her new life in Mount Hermon, and is familiar with the daily routines and duties. The year is punctuated by holidays and visits home but she is always happy to return to London. After the summer of 1937, Mair now faces a major decision: will she leave these shores and become a missionary or apply for a university place in the UK? Both choices are daunting but the odds of pursuing higher education are stacked against her. Not only are the costs steep but it is still relatively unusual for women, even though a growing number of universities are open to both genders. Her love of music and piano playing remain undiminished and she still cherishes the idea that one day she might still be a professional musician. So what should she do next?

CHAPTER 4

1938-39 Cardiff University

Mair's missionary ambitions are not realized after her two-year term at Mount Hermon. Maybe she feels she is too young for a life overseas in a distant colony, or more likely she carries a sense of responsibility for her father and little sister in Pontycymer. Spending time in London's most deprived areas has opened her eyes to the complexities of life and the sheer hard graft of being a young female missionary in a tough urban environment. She knows this isn't the time to make a lifelong commitment to such work.

Up to this point, and still only twenty, Mair has approached big decisions with clear focus and determination, but this time she isn't sure. Thus halfway through her time in Streatham, she applies to Cardiff University. Her higher examination results were very good and she decides to pursue her other great love, music. She enrols for the BMus (bachelor of music) degree and starts her studies in September 1938. Many arts degrees at that time require that students study subsidiary subjects, and Mair chooses German and history.

The University of South Wales and Monmouthshire opened its door for the first time on 24 October 1883. From the outset, this new university invited enrolments from men and women alike.

The highest value entrance scholarship offered to a student in the 1883 intake was made to a female student. This open-door policy towards women was further exemplified in 1904 when Millicent McKenzie was made the university's first female professor. She also became the first woman to be addressed as Professor in Britain, and the first woman member of the Cardiff Senate in 1904. This institution encourages bright women and is a perfect academic environment for Mair.

In 1885, the university's Aberdare Hall was opened, and was the first female hall of residence, allowing many more women access to the university. It is to Aberdare Hall that Mair comes in the autumn of 1938, and this will be her term-time home for the next three years. Although men are still in the overwhelming majority, she is now part of a growing and influential female cohort in the university.

This will be the last year of peace in Britain for some time. But while the news media reports daily accounts of international conflict, Mair is absorbed by her new environment and revels in her new freedom. She is able to play the piano whenever she chooses and strives to improve her technique. Even the thought of becoming a concert pianist surfaces again.

The music studios were beautiful; I'd never seen anything like them before. They were large and the acoustics were marvellous. I could play on a Steinway whenever I wanted to. On one of my first days, one of the rooms was empty and no one around. The piano was enormous and the wood gleaming. I only intended being in there for a couple of minutes but I started playing Beethoven's 'Emperor' concerto and I must have been playing for a quarter of an hour before looking up. I'd memorized this piece for my last exam

*and the luxury of playing it undisturbed was something I'd
not enjoyed for the last couple of years. This magnificent
instrument trembled and vibrated as I played softly and
then with passion. I was lost in the music and the moment.*

*Student life was quite the most wonderful thing. Because
I'd been to Mount Hermon I didn't feel any homesickness like
so many of the other girls felt. I was also two or three years
older than my peers so I wasn't as giddy as them either.*

Inevitably her interests lie in the university's small Christian Union,
affiliated to the Inter-Varsity Fellowship, or IVF as it is called.

*At that time it was a small group and really lacked
direction. The CU had dwindled in numbers and I just felt
that the people that were left were unnecessarily negative.
After I'd attended a few meetings, I realized it was the same
small group every time. Apart from me and my friend
Margaret it was all men. And we went through the same
routine of opening our Bibles, having a few prayers and
somebody would give an often dull talk.*

*It was clear to me that unless we started inviting some
new people, this group would be very short-lived. I felt I
had seen a different way of living as a Christian in London.
It was possible to make the message understandable and
attractive to all kinds of people, and there was no reason
why this couldn't happen in such a diverse and interesting
environment as the university. During a group discussion
I said that we should be thinking about reaching out to
people who weren't Christians with the simple message of
the Bible, and to do it in an organized way. After a few
weeks I was told that a new committee would soon be*

elected, and I was asked if I would object if my name was put forward. I was flattered by the offer and agreed. I was stunned to be elected in the first place and then the new committee voted me as the new first woman chair of the CU in Cardiff.

All this happens within a few weeks of Mair starting at university. This ability to get noticed and rise to sudden prominence has been a feature of her life from a young age, but this is a change from being the main pianist. In a largely conservative and male-dominated group, she somehow manages to become the leader of the pack. She has become, it seems, the first-ever female chair of the IVF in Britain.

But the growing anxiety of an impending global war is not lost on Mair. A month after she starts in Cardiff, world leaders gather in Munich to avoid conflict and prevent Hitler's Germany from invading Czechoslovakia. The Munich agreement is a great success for Prime Minister Neville Chamberlain. After landing in Heston airport he announces that he has in his hand a piece of paper, signed by Adolf Hitler; it promises "Peace in our time". There will be no Anglo-German war. The long disputed German part of Czechoslovakia, Sudetenland, will be ceded back to the Germans but there will be no invasion of the country. The policy of appeasement has triumphed for the time being.

But Mair is also aware of another conflict that predates events in eastern Europe. During a home visit to Dada and Beti, she hears about some miners who have gone abroad to fight.

For the last year or so I'd heard about the Spanish Civil War; a conflict between General Franco's nationalists and the Republicans. To be honest I hadn't give it much

*thought; it all seemed far away. I knew that Franco was a
fascist and that he had links with the Germans, but that's
about it. Dada told me that some of the men in the pit, big
union men, had actually gone to Spain to fight alongside
the Republicans. The trade union movement apparently
believed that this was a struggle for justice and equality
and that working men everywhere should be prepared to
join in the fight. They'd joined some international brigades
– a fancy name for troops, I think. To think that little
Pontycymer was now being represented in a European war!
Dada said these men had lost their jobs so presumably the
unions must have been supporting them. I felt I knew so
little about what was going on in the world and had buried
my head in the sand to some extent.*

In November 1938, disturbing anti-Semitic news comes out of
Germany. The assassination of an official in the German Embassy
in Paris by a French Jew elicits a brutal and disproportionate
response. Adolf Hitler issues a decree to the Gestapo, ordering
the invasion of all Jewish households and the destruction of
Jewish businesses. This night is known as Kristallnacht, the night
of broken glass. It is extensively covered in the newspapers and on
the radio. It also awakens Mair again to German aggression and
the vulnerability of the Jews.

I read The Manchester Guardian *and* The Times *in
the university library and felt sick after reading about
Kristallnacht. I'd met lots of Jewish people in Mount
Hermon and they were lovely, cultured people. How
could they be treated like this? And here I was studying
the German language. Many of the students thought the*

Germans were planning another war, to finish off what
they'd started in the Great War. I hoped they were wrong
but I'd heard Dada say the same thing.

Serious about her university career, Mair is earnest in her studies.
Lectures and seminars are attended, essays completed. And she
does hours of piano practice every day. Her hard work and talent
invite a positive response from the music professor, who urges
Mair to consider pursuing a career in music. But increasingly
her discipline and zeal is channelled into leading the largely
male Christian Union to a more outward-looking future. She is a
campaigner, an activist, and she has found a completely absorbing
cause. Away from the library, she is leading meetings, hosting
house parties and seeing the dwindling numbers increase. And
she's met John Russell-Jones, known as Russ.

A pleasant-looking man started coming to the meetings;
quite a few of the people knew him. He was confident and
was more comfortable speaking in Welsh than English. He
seemed to know a lot about literature and politics and I
can't say I liked him to begin with. I'd noticed him around
the campus a few times with a cigarette in his mouth. I
also knew that he was a member of the Student Christian
Movement which was a rival organization to our own.
They were known to be much more interested in political
issues than the IVF and also much more radical in their
understanding of the Bible. I'd read some of their literature
and they just weren't "sound", as I'd put it. Their views on
the Bible were not mine, arguing that it was a compilation
of texts that were important to the church but not inspired
in any way. That kind of talk made my blood boil.

*So when he came to our meeting the second time, I
said, "Who is this Russell-Jones?" to one of my friends.
She explained to me that he was training to be a Baptist
minister and came from West Wales. He was bright and
apparently a gifted preacher. I was icy towards him on
our first few meetings; truth be known I gave him quite a
grilling. I wanted to make sure he was genuine in his faith
and motives, only because I felt very protective of the group.
But his manner towards me was not argumentative or
hostile; he said that he shared the same views as I did. But
he also said that every argument has two sides and you had
to listen and understand both of them even if you disagreed
strongly with one of them.*

Their differences are many. Russ is politically alert and is
distrustful of any authority based on wealth or privilege. Mair
is instinctively more deferent and accepting of the given order.
As part of the celebrations marking his accession to the throne,
King George VI visits Cardiff and Mair recounts Russ's strange
memories of the occasion.

*Russ came really close to the king and queen when they
came to Cardiff in 1938. There'd been a large youth rally
in nearby Sophia Gardens and they'd come to the beautiful
civic centre, where the city hall, law courts and university
were located. When he saw them they were standing on
the steps leading to the museum. There must have been
thousands of people milling around and he saw them
standing there, outside the main entrance.*

*They looked awkward and ill at ease, especially the king.
He noticed that they both were heavily made up, even the*

*king! They seemed to be wearing a kind of white foundation
cream which gave them an eerie appearance. King George
was standing upright and nervous and his wife had a far-
away look in her eyes. They were so close to him, he could
have walked up to them and shaken them. There didn't
seem to be anyone looking after them; they seemed so lost.
Russ, of course, was very critical of them but I felt a kind of
sorrow for them. I read the later newspaper report that the
king and queen had been so happy to be in the Principality,
but happiness was not the emotion Russ observed that day.
I'd describe it more as a quiet terror. He looked like a man
who'd rather be anything than king.*

Despite this unpromising start in Mair's relationship with
Russ, a friendship is somehow birthed. Both are idealistic
in matters of faith, both Welsh speakers, and yet there is a
marked dissimilarity in their backgrounds. Russ is from an
impoverished home in Gorseinon, near Swansea. His father is a
foundry worker in the nearby tin works and a founding member
of the local Iron and Steel Trades Confederation lodge. Mair's
political education is right-leaning liberalism, cherishing social
justice but also encouraging a free market economy. Russ comes
from three generations of miners and steel workers, whose
movements can be traced across the South Wales valleys in sync
with the industrial revolution. Mair is from the landowning
classes; Russ belongs to the workers who formed unions and
took strike action, with bitter memories of the 1926 General
Strike. She believes in order and dogma; he is at home in the
world of ideas and causes. But both also come from close
families where education, chapel and Welsh culture give them a
close sense of affinity.

By the end of 1938, Russ is also on the IVF committee with Mair. Their relationship blossoms, not romantically but as comrades in a joint cause. They are on a mission to save the world, or at least the university. There are endless meetings, missions, church events, special speakers and yet more prayer meetings.

By the summer of 1939, Mair's main preoccupation, if not her obsession, is with the IVF. Most of her friendship group is drawn from the Christian Union. However, she does strike up a friendship with Helen, whose main degree is German. Since Mair's degree also involves studying this language they share lectures twice a week. Helen's father is a lecturer in the university and Mair visits the family's home several times. It is the very ordinariness and lack of spiritual intensity in this relationship that become increasingly important to Mair. Helen's life represents a space where she doesn't have to lead or campaign.

Under Mair's leadership, the Cardiff CU has grown from a small group of eccentric academics to one of the largest societies in the university, numbering over 200 members. The summer mission in Pontypridd is a high point. There's a buzz among the large student team; the people of the town respond well to the various events and meetings. They even arrange a tennis competition, which Mair inevitably wins.

But everything is about to change. On 23 August, Hitler and Stalin reach their first agreement. With Stalin now neutralized, Hitler feels free to invade Poland, and on 1 September he sends in his troops. The Munich agreement has already been broken with the occupation and dismantling of Czechoslovakia in March and this is now the final nail in the coffin of appeasement. This action by Adolf Hitler finally prompts Britain and France to discuss guaranteeing Polish independence and promising to oppose

Germany by military means if Poland is invaded. Within two days, Britain and France declare war against Germany.

*I remember the day vividly. It was Sunday 3 September;
a warm and sunny day of later summer. We didn't go to
chapel that morning as Dada said the prime minister was
making a speech that would be broadcast on the radio. At
11:15 we all gathered nervously around the wireless; the
three of us and most of the aunties too. The prime minister
sounded tired as he announced that we were now at war
with Germany. He said that this declaration was a bitter
blow to him and he felt defeated. I felt sorry for him but
the fear of war came into our little home and I think we
all felt it.*

After nearly a month of brutal fighting, the Polish forces surrender, and on 28 September the German–Soviet Treaty of Friendship is signed. There is no danger of Hitler having to fight a war on two fronts, and so, with Russia as his new ally, he can concentrate on dominating western Europe.

Before they return home for the Christmas holidays, Russ treats Mair to lunch in the Louis Restaurant in Cardiff's St Mary Street.

*It was a quaint, old-fashioned spot and very popular with
students. You could get a good meal for very little. I'm not
sure where Russ got the money from, but he always seemed
to have money on him. Strange that I came from quite a
wealthy background and never had any, but he could afford
to eat out and he was from a poor home! The waitresses,
all dressed in black with white aprons, were very attentive*

to us and they seemed to know Russ quite well. I felt quite special sitting there, but there was nothing between us – or nothing much. I liked his company and the way he spoke and thought so fluently but there wasn't really much more than that. He told me he'd given up smoking as he didn't think it was fitting for someone going into the ministry. I told him I agreed and that people would be looking to him as an example soon.

Most the time we talked about the war and how we felt about it. I asked him whether or not he would fight and I was surprised by the passion of his response. He said he was a pacifist and on no terms would he take arms to kill another human being, whatever the cause. He felt that as a Christian he might also end up killing other believers and this would be doubly wrong. We had a lively discussion, as we always did, and I countered him by arguing that we had to defend the Christian principles that had made Britain what it is. If no one did anything the enemy would come in and take away our freedoms, including religious freedom. He wasn't having any of it and started talking about Gandhi and someone called Toyohiko Kagawa. Kagawa was a Japanese theologian and, like Gandhi, advocated non-violent direct action. He'd been imprisoned several times for his radical views and led an anti-war movement.

In many ways we were so different. I became quite agitated with his attitude; it was too idealistic for me. I told him that if war was declared, then whatever everyone felt about it, we just had to get on with it. There would be a job to do and we would all have to play our part. He said that the church would have to stand up against warmongering and murder.

After a while, a jazz trio started playing and we stopped talking. Russ liked jazz, although it wasn't really my cup of tea. But it was lovely just listening to their music and just for a moment everything seemed normal. Despite our clash of views, I sensed there was a solid respect and trust between us – and maybe more than that.

Christmas 1939 is dominated by a dramatic royal radio broadcast by King George VI. Preparing the nation for the long and uncertain slog of war that is ahead of them, he quotes a poem called *The Gate of the Year*, written in 1908 by Minnie Haskins. Once again the Thomas family crowds around the wireless after the last Christmas meal before rationing bites.

He said the conflict was about defending Christian civilization and he referred to a poem which I'd never heard before, but it was really powerful and I memorized it. It went like this: "I said to the man who stood at the Gate of the Year, 'Give me a light that I may tread safely into the unknown.' And he replied, 'Go out into the darkness, and put your hand into the Hand of God. That shall be better than light, and safer than a known way.'" We were all quite emotional after the broadcast. I think everyone realized that the war was here to stay and nothing would be the same. This might even have been our last Christmas together. But we also felt strangely comforted by the king's speech. Dada and Mama too had been fond of the royal family, and that night it was as though we were part of one big family that was going to come through this together. I chuckled when I thought of Russ's likely reaction to this speech.

CHAPTER 5

1940 Too Close to Home

From the very beginning it was all going against us. It was hard keeping up with the war as very little was actually being reported, but it was obvious to everyone that Germany was in the saddle. They were powerful, knew what they were doing and it seemed as though they were going to sweep everyone away, including Britain.

The defeat of British and Allied troops in the battle of Norway in April is a huge blow to morale. German forces also invade Denmark under the noses of the British; a campaign supervised by the First Lord of the Admiralty, the Right Hon. Winston Churchill MP. Recognizing the need for greater cohesion and leadership, and having lost the confidence of most sides of the House, Neville Chamberlain resigns on 10 May and Winston Churchill becomes the new prime minister. Having served in both Liberal and Conservative governments, Churchill is a complex person and at this point not greatly loved or indeed trusted by the public. His arrival in the Commons on 13 May is greeted by thin applause and the Lords go a step further and welcome him with silence.

But he was the right man. Chamberlain, whom everyone
liked, had lost his authority. He didn't seem to have a
strategy to take the Germans on and we all wanted a
change. Even though Churchill wasn't popular in Wales
after he ordered the shooting of miners during some riots in
Tonypandy at the start of the century, we needed someone
with a bit of belligerence about them.

Germany's march across Europe is brutal. Victory in Norway and Denmark has been followed by triumph in Belgium, Holland and then France. In operation, strategy and downright cunning, the Germans are streets ahead of the Allies. Their squeeze on mainland Europe means that the British Expeditionary Force is driven back to Dunkirk where they are surrounded by German troops. Tens of thousands of British, French, Polish and Canadian troops are totally cut off, and are easy prey for their enemies. In one of the most unexplained episodes of the war, a rescue of epic proportions takes place. With General Paul von Kleist's Panzer division less than two miles from Dunkirk, Hitler issues an order that his troops must not enter the town. In the ensuing lull, Winston Churchill orders any available ship or boat to rescue the marooned soldiers. Over 900 vessels respond to this call of action, leading Churchill to describe it as "a miracle of deliverance". Between late May and early June 1940, nearly 339,000 troops, including thousands of French, are rescued in Operation Dynamo.

In one of his most memorable speeches to the House of Commons on 4 June 1940, Winston Churchill reflects on this strange retreating victory:

Even though large tracts of Europe and many old and
famous States have fallen, or may fall into the grip of the

Gestapo and all the odious apparatus of Nazi rule, we shall not flag or fail. We shall go on to the end. We shall fight in France, we shall fight on the seas and oceans, we shall fight with growing confidence and strength in the air, we shall defend our island, whatever the cost may be. We shall fight on the beaches, we shall fight on the landing grounds, we shall fight in the fields and in the streets, we shall fight in the hills, we shall never surrender. And if, which I do not believe, this island or a large part of it were subjugated and starving, then our Empire beyond the seas, armed and guarded by the British Fleet, would carry on the struggle until, in God's good time, the New World, with all its power and might, steps forth to the rescue and the liberation of the old.

The war was getting closer and closer. It was hard to believe that we might be invaded by another country but that's what was happening. It felt like we were sleepwalking into a terrible nightmare. If the Germans were that close, what could stop them landing on our shores? And there were so many rumours flying around. There were endless stories of German soldiers parachuting into the countryside dressed as nuns. In Wales there was a particular anxiety about the Germans arriving on our coast through Ireland, which was, of course, neutral during the war.

Away from these affairs of state, the IVF goes from strength to strength. Chairing a committee of six students, Mair has managed to turn the fortunes of this once-beleaguered group. Weekly meetings have record numbers in attendance and her ambition to see a well-argued and promoted Christian message on campus is bearing fruit. But these are straitened times. The new blackout measures result in the complete ban on any night-time public meetings. These take place in church halls during the daytime, mostly during afternoons or on Saturdays. And the committee has to meet wherever they can find; generally tea houses.

We particularly liked going to the Continental at the end of St Mary Street. There was plenty of space for us all. The manager knew who we were and was happy for us to stay for a while as long as we ordered tea. It was particularly memorable for its music and that's why we all liked it so much. We would time our visits so that once we'd got through our agenda, the small café orchestra would pipe up. They were really good and varied and appealed to most tastes. Mozart and Haydn were popular but they also played light classics and even some jazz on occasion. However, their playing always drew a crowd so we had to vary our meeting times and make way for paying customers. In many ways we were a funny little group of students. Some of us looked normal enough but there were one or two who looked most peculiar. I remember one young man, I can't remember his name, who wore heavy horn-rimmed round spectacles with very thick lenses. Whatever the weather, he wore a tightly bound long scarf wrapped around his neck. It always looked as though it was a snake and we were always teasing him.

Sadly their opening hours were greatly reduced halfway through 1940 and the orchestra was disbanded. We kept meeting there but somehow the atmosphere was never quite the same.

Virtually as soon as France surrenders to Nazi occupation in June, German attention turns towards Britain. On 10 July, the Battle of Britain begins – a term coined by Winston Churchill. The Luftwaffe begins its campaign for aerial domination. The war takes to the skies over Great Britain and Dada takes Mair and Beti for a day out to Porthcawl.

It was a blustery, fine day but not many people were about considering it was the summer holidays. People were nervous about bombs landing and so lots of people stayed inside. It was nice getting out of the valley and away from the aunties; it could all get rather oppressive. I asked Dada when he thought it would all end, and of course he didn't know. All he could say was the coal mine was now the busiest he had ever seen it, and the men were working around the clock to fulfil the government's orders. Welsh coal, apparently, was fuelling the war effort.

September comes and a new intake of students arrives at the university. Mair's campaigning zeal is limitless in hosting meetings, arranging guest speakers and recruiting new members for the IVF. She and her friend Margaret are in the library one lunchtime when they notice a new male student.

His name was Douglas Davies and he came from the Rhondda Valley. He was a shy young man and struggling to come to terms with university life. We invited him to a special meeting we'd arranged the following week, and he was glad to be invited and said he'd come.

Douglas Davies is also known as Glyn. It's a feature of Welsh family life that boys in particular are often given more than one Christian name; one by which they are generally known and the other for special occasions. To his family he is Glyn and to everyone else he is Douglas. Now ninety-two, this is his memory of that first meeting:

I came from Penygraig in the Rhondda Valley and came to Cardiff University to study Classics (Latin and Greek) and Welsh. In my first term I was working in the library when I was approached by two female students, Mair Thomas and Margaret Thomas. I think I had met them before and I understood later that they had been praying for me. They invited me to a Christian Union meeting where a guest speaker had been booked. I was interested and heard Dr Arnold Alldis speak. I became a Christian that night and this has been the greatest influence on my life since then.

Douglas becomes a regular member of the Christian Union and a strong friendship develops between him, Mair, and Russ. He is soon "doing his bit":

I never lived in halls of residence but commuted by train from home to Cardiff every day. Amazingly the trains ran on time every day; I don't remember any great delays or disruptions to the timetable. As soon as I started university I joined the ARP [Air Raid Precautions] as a fire officer, but it never experienced direct bombing attacks. I must say however that the best thing about being a fire officer was the enormous breakfasts you were given.

Russ is also a fire officer, along with other university friends. Some are volunteers while others are employed part-time. Set up in the months before the beginning of war, the ARP exists to protect civilians from the danger of air raids. The role is both precautionary and reactive. While Douglas is not involved in the aftermath of a major air strike or fire, others are not so fortunate. A friend of Russ's is a fire officer. Picking his way through the rubble of a blast, he discovers the grossly dismembered body of a child, limbs and torso ripped apart by the impact. He is to be continually awoken by the same nightmarish memory of this sight for the rest of his life.

As the year draws to a close, the tendrils of war are covering Britain, sucking life out of the population, leaving a suffocating sense of fear. Twelve months earlier there was great optimism that it would all be over within a matter of months; that right would overcome might. But those sentiments have crumbled against the German Axis and its successes.

Having conquered most of western and northern Europe, the German Luftwaffe wants to destroy the RAF before presumably making a land invasion. Their confidence levels are sky high. Hugely outnumbered in aircraft and personnel at the start of the battle, the Royal Air Force's abilities are severely tested.

The aerial aggression lasts from 12 August until 6 September. While the Royal Air Force has an operational capacity of 672 Spitfire and Hurricane fighters, the Luftwaffe numbered 3,272 bombers and fighters. By early September, however, the British number increases to 738 fighter planes. But the guile, strategy and barefaced grit of the air force under the direction of commander-in-chief of Fighter Command, Air Marshall Hugh Dowding outsmarts their German counterparts. Whereas Fighter Command loses 444 aircraft in one month, the German air force losses total more than 900, including bomber aircraft. Rather like the strange events of Dunkirk, the Germans seize defeat out of the jaws of victory at the Battle of Britain. Far from being the overwhelming victory expected by the Nazis, the conflict reaches stalemate.

By the middle of September, the Battle of Britain has switched from the airfields of the RAF to unremitting bombing attacks on Britain's key cities. On 15 September, there are huge raids on London, Southampton, Bristol, Liverpool, Manchester – and Cardiff. These sustained attacks last from the autumn of 1940 to spring 1941. As incendiary bombs scar and mutilate London and a host of other cities, the war falls from the skies and becomes a deadly street fight. Familiar people and buildings are destroyed. Such is the ferocity of the assault on London it is called the Blitz, shortening the German noun blitzkrieg; an intense military campaign intended to bring about a swift victory.

Mair is in her last year at Cardiff University and the final examinations are looming. In November she meets up with Dora Sanderson, a friend who is on leave and has returned home to Cardiff. During their conversation, Mair's eyes are opened to the war's dark secrets.

I met with Dora who was home on leave for a few days. She treated me to tea in the Continental and we were there for hours. The war, of course, dominated our conversation and we talked about the havoc and fear caused by the relentless bombing. We had both lived in London at different times and we became very nostalgic as we reminisced about the various landmarks that were probably no longer standing.

We'd only known each other a few months, but we really were the best of friends. She was working for the

Foreign Office in somewhere called Bletchley Park but she was very secretive about her work; wouldn't say a thing. But for some reason she started telling me how the Jews were being treated in Germany. I'd heard about the Kristallnacht in 1938 but for some reason or another I hadn't given it much thought since then. I started university at roughly the same time and was too busy with my own life. But Dora told me that it had got a lot worse. There were stories in the press about concentration camps being built where not only Jews but also Catholics and Poles and others were being treated like slaves. We also talked about the Nuremberg Laws which stripped Jews of their German citizenship and made it virtually impossible for them to find any kind of work.

I felt furious when I thought of what that man Hitler was doing. But she then said that the East End was filling up with Jewish people escaping persecution across Europe and it had been going on for years. It was as if my eyes opened to an ugly truth. I suddenly realized that I had met these people. I'd heard their stories but done nothing about it; I hadn't really paid attention. I knew they were fleeing the war but I hadn't reflected on the horrors those little children had witnessed. I was so immersed in my own adventures, I wasn't actually listening. But I did this afternoon. It felt like thick oily scales dropping off my eyes. This war was being waged against an innocent and helpless minority and somehow I needed to get involved.

From mid-December until the early days of the New Year, the weather in Britain is cold and bright. It would be perfect, under normal conditions, for a Christmas holiday, but now it is ideal for bombing and mass terror. People are wondering whether the Germans will take a break over Christmas.

Mair returns home to Pontycymer a few days before Christmas Eve and her thoughts are dominated by the future. Her relationship with Russ is now well established as a solid friendship. Both have strong Christian convictions, are active in the Christian Union and are at ease in each other's company. But is there more? Since the summer Mair senses their fondness for each other has changed. A new energy is pulling them together, laced with new feelings and desires. Unspoken, still formal in their encounters, Mair begins to wonder whether this man might one day be her husband.

Russ is training to be a Baptist minister, however, and this means that he has a further three years of study ahead of him. Mair has neither the ambition or patience for post-graduate study. And the thought of moving home and spending three years in a hidden valley with the world at war fills her with despair. Uncertain of the details, she knows that she wants once again to move away from home and play her part in the war effort.

Russ and Mair are at odds in their views on the war. Until this point, their disagreements have been largely academic but Mair is still reeling from her conversation with Dora. She now feels under constraint to do something positive to fight the enemy, but is aware that this may cause difficulties with Russ.

Russ was adamant that it is morally wrong to ever take anyone's life. He said governments did not have the right to order their citizens to take up arms against other humans, and he believed that killing another person was a sin that can never be justified, whatever the situation. His vociferousness really surprised me as he was normally such a mild-mannered man; but this was an issue that really made him very passionate and excited.

I could appreciate his argument but I didn't really agree with him. It seemed to me that Germany represented a threat to everything we held important, and if left alone Hitler would end up taking millions of innocent lives. Maybe war is a necessary evil in order to secure the freedom and peace of the world. Russ also accused me of being too pragmatic, but we were actually very different in our political views. He came from a family of socialists. My family was staunchly Liberal and Dada in particular was still very proud of the Lloyd George government during the First World War.

But Russ really was brave. Conscientious objectors were disliked by more or less everybody and they had to be pretty tough to withstand the anger and mockery that came their way. "Conchies" had to appear before a judge and tribunal and make their case. If successful they were ordered to do other work, such as being medical orderlies, but most of them lost their appeal and were commanded to fight. A few were imprisoned for not complying with the court tribunal.

Russ wanted to stand up and be counted but he couldn't. He'd been given exemption as a clergyman, even though he was only studying to be one. He later heard that his parents had been given a hard time by neighbours, accusing them of having a coward as a son. He said that had he known this at the time he would have reconsidered his position.

But their relationship isn't exclusively about high-minded principles. In November, the Capitol cinema in Cardiff hosts a few showings of *Fantasia*, the new blockbuster from Walt Disney. Featuring a brand new character, Mickey Mouse, the film's soundtrack is rich in classical music. Russ takes Mair, and the evening proves to be memorable.

I wasn't used to going to the cinema and neither was Russ, but the film was mesmerizing. The combination of beautiful music and sensational imagery was breathtaking. We also drew even closer that night. We didn't hold hands but I linked my arm through his on the way back to Aberdare Hall and it felt wonderful.

Mair's homeward journey that Christmas is full of mixed feelings. Russ has returned to his family and she knows she needs to be with her father, still grieving his wife's death nearly six years ago. But since leaving home as an eighteen-year-old, her associations with the valley and her wider family have become less important. She feels different. Her Christian zeal has not ebbed and neither has her appetite for life. She's left wondering what may be waiting for her after next May's finals.

The dying weeks of 1940 sees Britain attempting a happy Christmas amid the growling of bombs. Thanks to a government directive, only unusually small Christmas trees are available. These dwarf trees will be less visible, apparently, to the German enemy. Hard to see how they will threaten national security, given that mandatory blackouts are now in force.

This year's Christmas celebrations are conducted under the canopy of warfare.

It was a strange and quiet Christmas that year. Pontycymer was blacked out and empty and I can't say it was a pleasant holiday period. There was very little in the shops, food was now rationed and people either didn't have the money to spend or the appetite to go out and buy. Even the church bells were quiet; it was eerie. We didn't go to chapel either, adding to the strangeness of the day. With so many men away at war, no one met to worship on this special day. This just added to the sense of unreality.

Dada, Beti and I went for walk on the hills while Aunty Jane cooked Christmas dinner. It was a beautiful, sunny and crisp day but I felt we were spectators… I felt I was in a trance, disconnected from what should have been a happy occasion. Some of our neighbours had lost sons in the naval conflicts and no one felt like celebrating. Aunty Jane, dressed in her customary black from head to toe, served us a meal of baked rabbit with a few vegetables, followed by suet pudding. Beti was happy enough but Dada's grief filled the house in Bryn Cerdd. But despite it all, my darling Dada's heroic generosity shone through and he gave Beti and me soap as presents!

A few days later and Mair is leafing through Dada's copy of the *Western Mail* newspaper.

The newspapers were full of reports and photographs of the Blitz. It had been going on for months and months. London was hit badly, and many of the areas I knew when I lived there only three years earlier had been torn apart. The Strand had apparently been hit. I had such fond memories of getting off the train at Charing Cross and spending the day walking around Trafalgar Square and the National Gallery; not to mention the wonderful Lyons tea house on the Strand.

Air raid sirens sounded across the valley that night, and we spent a nervous few hours fumbling with our gas masks in the cwtch *near the piano room at home in Pontycymer.*

There were no Andersen huts in the Garw Valley as you had to be wealthy and have a large garden to house one of these. Most people fled to crowded public shelters, but after 1940 a cheaper indoor alternative was introduced. The Morrison shelter was a large table with wire mesh sides. During the day it served as a table and during air raids it was possible to sleep underneath it. But I don't think it was all that popular.

On 29 December, the family tunes into the BBC Home Service and hears news of a devastating air strike; London is on fire.

The news was getting worse and the bombing in London more intense. The newscaster said that Londoners had not seen anything like this since the Great Fire in Samuel Pepys's time. Aldersgate, Cheapside and Moorgate were all burning. Some of the city's oldest and most beautiful churches built by Christopher Wren had been destroyed. There was a large Jewish ghetto in that area; it was where I used to go every week when I was in Mount Hermon. I heard that Shoreditch had been hit; I used to teach at a Jewish school there and now it had probably been obliterated. So far the skies over Wales had been silent, but it felt like the Germans were getting ready for a big push. I was reminded of something Dora had said to me recently. She knew people who acted as volunteer ambulance drivers, driving around the East End and digging people out of the debris. Some of them would be dead, others nearly dead and the rest often in severe pain. It was a macabre job, like something out of Dickens's Hard Times, *but I couldn't help thinking about those people when the bombs were falling on London.*

CHAPTER 6

FEBRUARY 1941 Strange Messengers

In February, Wales witnesses further bombing raids. Swansea again bears the brunt of the attack over a period of three days. Mair has returned home for a weekend break and she recalls hearing the drone of the aircraft.

Dada, Beti, Aunty Jane and I sat in the cwtch *braced for the dreadful screams, whistles and bangs of the bombs. Even if you were miles and miles away you felt the force of the thud right inside you. I heard them coming over the Garw, right overhead! There was that familiar blast, shaking and feeling of being sick right in the pit of you. For some reason or another they must have dropped a bomb on the top of the mountain.*

I pitied the people who were going to get the full force of this. We had three nights of it.

The Three Nights Blitz in February 1941 lasts for seventy-two hours and is the most sustained bombardment outside London. Curiously, Swansea's docks and heavy industries are barely touched but the town centre is completely flattened. The Luftwaffe unleashes 1,273 high explosive bombs and 56,000 incendiary devices to devastate an area of 41 acres. Over 857 properties are destroyed, and a further 11,000 damaged. Yet again the death toll is savage: 230 people are killed and more than 400 injured.

Surprisingly, some of the city's oldest buildings, the Castle, Swansea Museum, and the Glynn Vivian Art Gallery survive, but the town's commercial heart is torn apart and the Ben Evans department store, which seemed to have supplied everyone with everything for upward of fifty years, is flattened.

Further clarity regarding her future comes to Mair in March after two connected but strange encounters. As her final examinations loom and the bitterly cold winter yields to a warm spring, her hours are increasingly spent in the university library. While she is confident in German and music, history is her bête noire. Memorizing and analyzing past events are not part of her nature. She was and remains a pragmatist; a woman for whom present challenges are always more urgent than reflecting on past events. Thus her library hours are dominated by attempts to master the historian's art.

> *I couldn't be doing with all those endless dates and analysis. Music was instinctive and you knew where you were with German; it was a matter of syntax, grammar and following the rules. History was a strange mix of facts and opinion and I simply couldn't get on top of it.*

During one quiet afternoon among the books and journals she receives a tap on her shoulder.

*I turned round and there was a man standing above me;
a nice-looking man wearing a dark tweedy kind of suit.
He must have been in his thirties. As soon as he started
talking I could tell he wasn't from Wales; it's what you'd call
received English. It was the kind of accent you'd hear on the
BBC. He told me he was from the Foreign Office. In fact,
that's all he said about himself. He didn't give me his name
or anything.*

*It became very clear, however, that he knew a great deal
about me, or at least a few very specific things. He said
he'd heard I was very good with languages and puzzles,
and would I like to try out for a top secret project? To be
quite honest I didn't know what to say. I hadn't met this
man before, didn't recognize him at all; he was the classic
tall, dark stranger! The thought of working for the Foreign
Office really struck a chord inside me, though. It sounded
important, serious, and, if I'm honest, a little bit glamorous.*

*I asked him a few more questions but he became
more and more guarded. He said that I would be solving
problems and using my language skills for the country.
He didn't say where or when, but he did stress it was all
very hush hush and I'd need to keep a secret. I wouldn't
be allowed to tell anyone, not even my family. This
conversation was quite disturbing but it definitely drew me
in and I said that I would be interested in this project. He
said that I should write to the Foreign Office in Whitehall
and express my interest. With that, he turned and left the
library. Even now as I look back on that encounter, it seems
most peculiar. But it was the war and nothing was normal
in those days.*

Mair muses over this encounter for the next week but does not act on it. The prospect of working for the Foreign Office is intriguing and attractive. It would certainly address the uncertainty of her post-university life but she's unsure. The strangeness of the meeting and the vagueness of the invitation of writing to no one in particular in Whitehall prevent her from taking it any further.

Without any apparent connection, her friend Dora Sanderson pops up again in the next few weeks. Mair's relationship with Dora had begun at a student Christian event some months earlier. Even though Dora came from Cardiff, she had studied modern languages at London University and is now working for the Foreign Office. Her meeting Mair at this time is crucial, although the focus of their relationship is the war and their response to it.

Dora was back in Cardiff and this time she came to see me in Aberdare Hall. She was a quiet, controlled woman but I wouldn't call her shy; in fact, she was strong, steely, and quietly confident. She never talked about her parents or whether she had any siblings. We chatted about the war and how terrible it was all looking at the time. She said that Churchill had the right ideas and that we shouldn't be bullied into submission by the Germans.

Somehow or another we started talking about her work at the Foreign Office. She told me that she was using her language skills and it related directly to the war effort, but she didn't tell me the nature of her work or where she did it. I tried pressing her further but she said it was top secret and she was forbidden to say any more. She said that they were looking for bright graduates and that I should write to the Foreign Office and ask for a job. But when I said that I didn't know what job to apply for, she said that it didn't matter as they would know what I was talking about! It felt as though Dora was talking in riddles. But the little she told me kindled a flame of excitement and I replied that I would probably write to the Foreign Office. I then described to Dora my encounter with the tweeded gentleman in the last few weeks. I recounted our strange and brief conversation and remarked how similar it had been to our chat that afternoon.

If Dora knew anything about my rendezvous with that man she passed no comment, and looked back at me with a kind of benign smile. But, of course, that was the point of whatever it was she was doing; keeping secrets. I tried pressing her again for more information about where she worked and lived, what sort of things she did. But she just wouldn't take it any further. In fact the only two definite disclosures she made were that she worked for the Foreign Office and she had signed the Official Secrets Act.

Many decades have drifted by since this period, but it still seems very strange – two apparently unconnected conversations, one of which involves a stranger for whom this is his only appearance in Mair's life… The encounter fits snugly into a John le Carré novel, but espionage must of necessity be odd and secret. And, of course, secrecy was the name of the game. These incidents also explain a routine response that my mother repeats over and over during my childhood. When anyone asks what part she played in the war, she always says the same thing: "I worked for the Foreign Office." What she had received from Dora and the tall dark stranger she passes onto us. She learned well.

Apparently neither of these two characters knew each other, but that's straining credulity. These were extraordinary times and troops were being mustered to fight on the intelligence front. Mair's curiosity was kindled by these approaches. In fact, her response was vocational; she felt she had to pursue the matter.

It felt like I had been given a sense of purpose, something to do. Up to this point there were plenty of options I didn't want to take, like going home or staying on in university, but I had no positive direction. Dora's few words about her work intrigued me and the thought of working for the Foreign Office was exciting. I had enjoyed my two years living in London and I suppose I wanted to reacquaint myself with the place and be in the centre of everything.

And so Mair writes a letter of application for an unknown post to an unnamed member of staff at the British and Foreign Commonwealth Office in Whitehall. Within a week she receives a reply. It's from a Miss Moore, based in St James's Street, Whitehall, London SW1, thanking Mair for her application and inviting her to an interview after Easter. The letter is polite, brief and gives directions. The duration of the interview will be one hour and she will be told whether or not she has a job on the day.

CHAPTER 7

APRIL 1941 Appointment in Whitehall

In April, Mair and Russ take a train to London for Mair's interview. According to her letter from Miss Moore she is to be at the British and Foreign Commonwealth Office at 3 p.m. This is Mair and Russ's first full day together. In order to make the most of the day, they're on the 7 a.m. train, which will take them about four hours to get to London.

It was the nicest day. I'd bought a new frock and shoes and Russ wore a smart suit. Even though all the carriages were full, we managed to find a couple of seats and we chatted and laughed most of the way to Paddington. There were so many soldiers travelling, but the atmosphere was surprisingly happy; you wouldn't have thought we were in the middle of a dreadful war. By the time we got to London the sun was out and the air was warm.

London was in a sorry state. Everywhere we saw bombed buildings and debris. And I mean everywhere. Somehow people were getting around, but the devastation was painful to see. Russ hadn't been to London before and I wanted to show him around, but nothing looked the same.

We got a bus to St Paul's and I was thankful it was still standing, but it was surrounded by ruins. Inside the church it was as if nothing had happened. It was serene. Even Russ thought it the most striking building he'd been in – quite an admission for a Baptist! It was much worse to the east of St Paul's; entire neighbourhoods had been razed to the ground, according to the bus conductor. I felt a lump in my throat when I thought of those happy days in Mount Hermon only three years before. We walked through the city and it was busy but there were ruined buildings everywhere. When we got to Liverpool Street, I remembered that Cable Street was near there; the scene of the awful fascist riots. I persuaded Russ we had enough time to make a detour and I took him to the scene. That part of London looked ravaged by war. Whole streets had been bombed and remained derelict; some had been shored up but most were exposed to the elements and curious people. Some of the precarious buildings were being used by Londoners who would be otherwise homeless.

Standing in Cable Street I tried to imagine the confrontation that took place there between Oswald Mosley's extreme right wing followers and the ordinary residents of the East End. Even though I had not witnessed any of it, it struck me that what happened there was an anticipation of the war itself. Somehow or another, this revolting political philosophy had infected the heart and minds of angry people and given them an ugly cause to believe in. Russ said he'd seen a newsreel film of the riots, but standing there made him realize the scale of the episode. I said that we had to beat this cancer of anti-Semitism and match fire with fire. Russ very wisely did not reply; I fear we would have had an open-air argument and not an open-air meeting.

We had a snack lunch near Piccadilly; I was too nervous by now to eat much. I thought about my conversations with Dora and my application letter to the Foreign Office and it all seemed a bit bare. I knew virtually nothing about the post I'd applied for, and here I was, about to have an interview for which I couldn't prepare. We made our way towards Whitehall but we were far too early, so we sat in St James's Park. There was blossom and colour everywhere and a subtle scent of life and vitality. In that little enclave of the city all we could hear was the sound of birdsong and the dull trudge of footsteps on the gravel paths. No cars, buses, and neither was there that smell of burning that we'd encountered up at St Paul's. It was the kind of heavy, acrid aroma that makes you want to clear your throat all the time. But the air was clean here. Despite everything, Whitehall and the Houses of Parliament had escaped destruction. And we were so happy in each other's company; content in being together. I didn't feel I had to speak all the time to fill in the gaps; we were at ease with each other.

As soon as I entered the Foreign Office, I felt completely overwhelmed; this was grandeur on a sumptuous scale. The ceilings were vaulted and vast landscapes and portraits hung on the walls. I felt very small. "What's a girl from Pontycymer doing here?" I thought to myself. I reported to the main desk and waited for my appointment. I heard the clip clop of heels on the marble floor and I knew this was for me. The heels belonged to a middle-aged lady called Miss

*Moore. She was pleasant but serious and wore her hair
in a bun. I followed her to a bland and cramped office in
comparison with the surrounding splendour.*

*She asked me a few questions about my degree, music and
German in particular. I was waiting for a written test but
none came. We talked about the war and she began speaking
about the importance of gathering intelligence in defeating
the Germans. She said that they were looking for graduates to
work in a new unit they had established in Buckinghamshire.
It was called Bletchley Park and I would be based there. The
purpose of this new department was to intercept and crack
the codes the Germans were sending to their frontline troops.
It was called the Government Code and Cypher School, but
no one could ever know about it, and neither could I tell
anyone about my work. My only satisfaction would be that
I had helped in the British war effort.*

*She then asked me if I wanted the job. I was tempted to
ask what job, but I didn't. Instead I said yes and she ferried
me down the corridor to another office. This was much more
formal in a military kind of way. There were maps on the
walls and, in the middle, a large table covered in a tablecloth
around which sat three army officers. They barely looked at
me. There was a document on the table. Miss Moore asked
me to sit down and she picked up the document. "This," she
said, "is the Official Secrets Act. As a government official
you are obliged to sign it and it is a binding legal document.
If you disclose your work at Bletchley Park to anyone, you
will be in breach of this and the consequences could be
serious, and could even include imprisonment."*

*My work would be confidential and I had to keep this
secret for the rest of my life. I would be handling highly*

sensitive information and I was to trust no one; not even my own family. After her little speech, the officers continued to ignore me but she asked me again if I wanted the job. I repeated my acceptance and signed the Official Secrets Act in the presence of these four witnesses.

I was elated and despondent at the same time. This would be a great opportunity to do something useful and might even produce an interesting career in the future. But I knew there would be difficult consequences flowing from this decision.

When I walked back into the sunshine and St James's Park, Russ was waiting for me. But now there was something I couldn't tell him; it felt like a heavy weight. I told him I had signed the Act and fair play, he didn't ask any more questions.

Mair is largely silent on the journey back. They decide to go back to Pontycymer so she can tell her father. Sitting in the familiar living room she makes a crucial decision, but not before a tense conversation.

Russ and I had barely spoken all the way back from London. I was full of contradictory feelings and didn't know what to do with them all. I had signed that blessed Act and I couldn't say a word to him, but I desperately wanted to. I needed his wisdom and insight, although actually it was too late for that anyway. I had accepted the job and signed my life away. This war could go on for years to come, and how would this affect our relationship? I knew that he knew we would be man and wife one day. This decision might have a direct impact on our future relationship, and what about

Dada? I had already left him twice to go to London and then university; this didn't seem at all fair. Beti was still young and living at home, and I couldn't help feeling that she was resentful of my time away from home. Would this new and indefinite posting put greater pressure on her to look after Dada while I moved away to Buckinghamshire?

It's very odd, but we sat in silence to begin with. They were waiting for me to say something and I was too full of emotion to know what to say or how to say it. In the end Dada asked me if I'd made my mind up. I don't know why, but I reacted badly to this. I told him that I couldn't tell him anything and if he had any idea what I was facing, he wouldn't ask such a silly question. Poor Dada went very silent, as did Russ. I then burst into tears and apologized. As I sniffled and cried, I told them that I had accepted a post in the Foreign Office and would be posted away from Wales in the next couple of months. All this emotion flooded out of me and I told Dada I was sorry that I was leaving him again and hoped I wasn't being selfish. I also said I hoped this wouldn't quash any of Beti's ambitions to move on with her life.

Dada had tears in his eyes by now, but he took me by the hand and told me that I must go and serve my country and that, whatever it was, it must be very important. I needn't worry about Beti; he was keen for her to go on to further studies but she had chosen not to, against his wishes. He hoped one day she would change her mind, but whether I stayed at home or left, it would have no bearing on her future plans.

The sun was setting and we were sitting in the shadows of the day in our living room. I heard the front door open *and in came Beti, surprised to see us all looking so glum and serious. She could see I'd been crying and bless her, she just knelt down and gave me a big hug without saying anything. I explained to her that I had been offered the job and accepted it. She looked worried and uncertain, but still she didn't say anything. She gave me another hug and a peck on the cheek before leaving the room. I know she believed me, but all this cloak and dagger secrecy was too much for her.*

Back in the company of her father and Russ, Mair decides that she needs to disclose a bit more than she's probably allowed to.

These were the two men I trusted most in my life. I was in a real quandary. I had signed the Official Secrets Act and couldn't say anything, but on the train home I had been trying to work out what I could say without being in breach of it. In the end, I told them that I had been offered a post working for the Foreign Office in a place called Bletchley Park in Buckinghamshire. This was top secret work and I would be handling very confidential intelligence about German operations. I would be leaving [for BP] after I finished university and would be based there for as long as the war lasted. My voice was shaking and I felt overwhelmed by what I was saying. As I bit back the tears I asked them to keep this completely confidential. No one must ever know where I was or what I was doing. The tears were flowing and Russ, bless him, took my hand in front of Dada and suggested we had a word of prayer. He prayed God's peace and blessing on us and asked that we all be faithful to God's purposes, however the future unfolded.

The following day, Aunty Lucy arrives at the house, eager for more information. Beti has relayed the details of Mair's new post but she wants to know more than this.

I stuck to the script that I had developed; I would be working for the Foreign Office in the London area, but I couldn't say any more as I had the signed the Official Secrets Act. Her response was horrid. She told me not to be so silly. How could a girl like me be employed by the government in such a responsible job when I hadn't done much with my life? Not for the first time with Dada's family, I saw red and said more than I should have. I had studied in London and Cardiff; more than her Edward had ever done. This was a real job and I would be serving the country and I would have thought she would be happy for me. She left the house soon afterwards, but our relationship never really improved after this.

After a few days at home, Mair returns to Cardiff to prepare for her final examinations. Her remaining two months at university show a change in attitude and she has lost the sharpness of her previous academic appetite. She arrived as an ambitious and focused student, determined to gain the best degree possible. But her mind is now conflicted, trying to mull over the many changes that she is facing. Long revision hours in the library leave her feeling unable to remember anything and she's not sleeping properly. Faced with the momentous and secret duties ahead of her, she is cramming for a degree that now seems pointless. However, she completes her finals, is informed that she has been successful, but does not see the fruit of all her hard work.

I wasn't able to attend the graduation ceremony as I had left Cardiff at that point. My new employers told me it wasn't important enough for a day's leave and my new duties were now of greater significance. They told me I was lucky to have graduated at all as there were many people working in BP who had been taken away from their studies before sitting their finals. I thought this was a fabrication at the time, but it proved to be true. A lot of people working in BP had had their studies disturbed and I can only assume that they returned to university after the war. I know I was awarded a B.Mus with honours, but to this day I still don't know what class of degree I gained.

After my finals, the endless goodbyes to aunts, uncles, family and friends started. I was bound for BP at the beginning of August, and the intervening weeks were a blur of meetings and trying to plan for the unplannable. We had all hoped at the start of it all that the war would be over within a year, but I now knew I might also spend the rest of my days in Buckinghamshire. We all knew that we were up against a very committed enemy, and how or when this conflict would end was by no means certain.

Leaving Russ was the worst part of it all, harder than even saying goodbye to my dear Dada. At that time we were walking out with each other, but we were still tentative about the future. We both wanted to do the right thing, especially as our faith was important and we wanted to be sure that our relationship was built on the right foundations. Our friendship seemed to be taking a different direction and our feelings for each other were getting more intense. What had started with caution, and a certain amount of suspicion on my part, had bloomed into a lovely and trusting comradeship. But the promise of romance was not far away; there was a physical and emotional chemistry between us and I think we both knew it and didn't know what to do about it.

We both recognized, however, that we were very different in some respects, while also sharing the same outlook on life. I was really clear about my faith and he seemed so diplomatic about his convictions. And he was so Welsh, clearly more nationalistic than anyone else in the CU. Even though I'd been brought up to speak Welsh, the world to me was much bigger than this country. I soon realized that we both shared the same deep spiritual convictions, and there was a high level of trust between us, right from the beginning.

I was more open about things, happy to share my opinions with others, and believed in the power of persuasion. Russ was more bookish, better at listening to people who didn't agree with him and respecting their views. He was less argumentative than me and seemed able to tolerate differences of opinion, whereas I was convinced of the rightness of my position. And I would argue the toss even if I knew I was on shaky ground!

Russ could be equally dogmatic, however, with people whom he thought should know better. So with other ministers he would react with great verbal force if he felt they were wrong on some piece of doctrine or interpretation of the Bible. There were times, and they weren't often, when he would be prepared to jeopardize a friendship if he felt the principle at stake was sufficiently important. But these occasions were very few and, because most of the people he fell out with all spoke Welsh and shared the same *backgrounds, this culture acted as a magnet in bringing them all back together again. Once or twice I heard him and his fellow student ministers argue in the Baptist college common room and it was as rowdy as anything that went on in parliament.*

He was also very kind and tender-hearted. He felt so deeply about other people and I loved him for this. He was cut out for church ministry, but I couldn't see then that we would take that journey together. He was now studying for his second degree in divinity, and although we were seeing less of each other, we both knew instinctively where this was heading. We had fallen in love and we both knew, deep down, that we would marry, but this seemed a long time in the future.

Chapter 8

August 1941 My Longest Day

The day when I had to leave for BP eventually came, and even though it was August, it was a grey and dank farewell at the bus station in Pontycymer. Dada, Beti and I walked down there for me to catch the bus to Bridgend. I had dressed rather optimistically for the journey, wearing a light frock and blazer. It was actually quite chilly and I felt cold inside.

I was really pleased that I had a good job waiting for me and the money would certainly help, but Dada looked very frail that morning as we said our goodbyes. Mama had died six years earlier and he looked very alone that day. It's funny what you remember, but he was wearing a raincoat even though it wasn't raining. It was as though he was still clothed in grief somehow. He had been upset when I left for Mount Hermon in 1936 and now he was still very emotional. He was pleased that I had found work but he was obviously distressed. I don't think he was unhappy with my decision, but he was unhappy with the way life had turned out for him.

My sister Beti was the complete opposite. She had met Don and was happy in love. She too had been very tearful when I left for Mount Hermon, and also quite cross with me. Mama hadn't long passed away and Beti wanted her big sister around the home. All my aunties had felt the same way, although Dada, strangely enough, had again been right behind me. Beti just thought I was being selfish. But this time everything was different for her. She was distracted by her exciting new life. The weather must have been colder than I recall because Beti was wearing a stylish woollen coat with a belt. It was certainly windy because her strawberry blonde hair was windswept and she looked a bit like Bette Davis!

The bus was red with a cream stripe. It had Western Welsh scrawled in large gold italics on its side, the biggest bus company in South Wales. You could travel anywhere with Western Welsh. Eventually the idling engine revved up and we pulled away from the bus station. I remember the racket it made; the shuddering vibrations and smell of fumes. I lost sight of Dada and Beti and we rumbled down the high street, passed Palledri's café and Mama's old shop and headed towards Bridgend. The bus's jerky braking and irregular speeds were taking me further from my lovely man in Cardiff.

For the third time in my life I was leaving this hidden valley, and this time it could be for good. I realized I had no idea where I was going. I knew the name of the village to which I was travelling but it meant nothing to me. I had never been to Buckinghamshire in my life and it felt very distant, a long way from little Wales. Even though I had lived in London for two years and could find my way

*around the East End, this seemed very different. I thought
to myself, "Mair, you don't know where you're going or what
you'll be doing!"*

*Sitting there, staring out at the familiar streets of the
Garw Valley, I began to feel very lonely. Was I doing the
right thing? Unlike my interview in Whitehall where
Russ accompanied me, I was travelling on my own. I was
expressly forbidden from having anyone else with me, and
my letter of appointment informed me that this was a top
secret mission and that no one must know my whereabouts
– no one at all. That's very hard especially when you like to
be as open about everything as I am.*

The bus pulls into the railway station in Bridgend, and the place
is bustling with travellers. Built for a more genteel and quieter
Victorian era, there are military personnel everywhere, and
the car park is congested with all manner of service vehicles.
Mair books her ticket to Bletchley and is soon in a second-class
carriage seat.

*The railway station at Bridgend was heaving with people
and the train was also packed. The effort of navigating my
way around so many people squeezed my emotions out of
me, but I knew that going to BP was the right decision. I've
always been like that. No matter what the pressure is, once
I make my mind up about a decision, I rarely have regrets. I
had decided to accept this job and that was that.*

*The carriages were full of people, mostly men, in
uniforms. Journeying to new postings, returning on leave,
or simply moving around as part of their duties; more or
less everyone was involved with the business of war. I had to*

stand for a while but eventually a kind man beckoned me over and gave up his seat for me. Even though we were at war, people didn't forget their manners. More people joined us in Cardiff and it was unbearably stuffy, even though the windows had been opened. Having said that, once we got going at full pelt, the fresh air and smell of steam filled the whole train. And I thought: "You're part of this enormous team that's going to defeat the Nazis." I began to feel the adventure of it all.

The aftermath of the Blitz could be seen everywhere. It didn't hit coal mining areas like the Garw Valley, although I do remember hearing the roar of the Luftwaffe high above Pontycymer in 1940 on their way to bombing Cardiff or Swansea, probably. I was familiar with the wreckage I'd seen in Cardiff, but as we pulled into Temple Meads station in Bristol, I hadn't realized how badly that city had been devastated. Back in those days we grew accustomed to seeing rubble and destruction everywhere. Where once there had been houses, offices or roads, there were now these vast piles of rubbish. And you'd nearly always see children playing nearby, showing how creative they can be even in the midst of carnage! Swindon and Didcot had been bombed too, but Oxford still looked pretty and unspoilt. Amazing, really, when you think about all the treasures on show in that city.

Sitting opposite Mair is an elderly gentleman, his attentions deep in the pages of *The Times*. On the front page, which Mair reads, is a short story about the number of Jews fleeing Germany, and concerns about their alleged persecution.

Ever since my time in Mount Hermon, and after my conversation with Dora in Cardiff, I was exercised about the condition of the Jews. There were all sorts of rumours circulating about their mistreatment and I didn't know what to believe. I found it hard to accept that a state would pick on one ethnic group, but the stories of flight from persecution were being reported regularly. It was as though the press knew more than they were letting on. And when I thought about pacifism's response, my blood boiled. Doing nothing in the face of a monster like Adolf Hitler was a hopeless response. Anyway, Russ and I agreed to disagree, and here I was on my way to a job I couldn't talk about but that would have a direct impact on the war. I've always believed that the people of Israel are special.

During the writing of this book, Mair has repeated the same request on too many occasions to remember.

Don't forget about the Jews. They were being treated terribly, but none of us knew how badly until the war had ended. But I'd seen something of their plight in my Mount Hermon years, and the vile picture fell into place once Germany was defeated.

She harbours a mixture of injustice and guilt over the issue of the treatment of the Jews; a sense that they were grossly abused during the war and that the Allies probably knew more than they were prepared to admit, all borne out of a conviction that this is the Bible's ancient and special people, to whom a debt is owed. Her feeling of guilt is stronger. She witnessed the thousands of European Jewish migrants pouring into the compact streets of the

East End prior to the war, and didn't make the connection with Nazism until 1941. Reason asserts that her intervention at any point would have carried no weight; she saw what many others were seeing. But the voice of emotion is so loud she believes that she could have done something to alter the course of their tragic journey. There's unfinished business, matters to resolve, and maybe in giving her account she will convince herself that she could not have done any more.

The weather was overcast when I left Pontycymer, and it started raining the further east we travelled. By the time we arrived in Bletchley that evening it was grey and drizzly. So much for the long, warm summer evenings we'd been enjoying; the weather that day was cold and miserable. I was trying very hard to remain positive, but I felt far away from everything that was familiar. I also knew that if I thought too much of home I would start crying and no good would come of that. But this wasn't the end of my journey, not today at any rate.

It was nearly dark, twilight if the skies hadn't been so cloudy, so it must have been about eight o'clock in the evening when I walked out of the station. It was strangely quiet, much less activity than Bridgend station where my day had started. I even wondered if maybe I'd come to the wrong place. I had assumed that BP would dominate everything around here and that the railway station would reflect that busyness. But there was hardly anyone around. I did, however, see a few people struggling with bags and cases, looking as solitary as me. I wondered if they too were bound for the secrets of Bletchley Park, but I was too wary of approaching anyone lest I might give away some vital piece of information and breach the confidentiality I had sworn.

From what I could see, the station was Victorian and fading, just like all the other railway stations I had been to. It had light yellow stonework, broad platforms and a feeling of being in a draughty cavern.

I'd been told to settle into my new lodgings a day before starting work at Bletchley Park, at an address in somewhere called New Bradwell. I changed platforms for the local branch line and waited for the steam engine that would take me a few miles north of Bletchley to the home of a Mr and Mrs Hill.

CHAPTER 9

AUGUST 1941 Landlords from Hell

It was the flattest place I had ever been to. I was used to mountains. And the accent was unusual: a mixture of East End London and presumably rural Buckinghamshire. It was a strange location, hard to know where it actually belonged. It wasn't the south-east, but neither was it the Midlands. Somebody described it to me as west Anglia and they were probably right.

BP employees are billeted across an area of north Buckinghamshire now known as Milton Keynes and beyond. A few are accommodated in hotels, pubs and guest houses, even in the splendour of Woburn Abbey. But most are given lodgings or "digs" in private homes in the villages and towns of Fenny Stratford, Wolverton, Stony Stratford, New Bradwell, Deanshanger, and Newport Parnell as well as Bletchley. Military personnel in BP are accommodated in various camps including a base in Bedford, some twenty miles to the east.

There are significant financial incentives for homeowners with spare rooms willing to take in these mysterious new tenants. It isn't much of a choice, however. Hefty financial penalties await those who decline this opportunity, while those who consent will receive generous extra allowances for food. The agreement between lodger and landlord, brokered by the Foreign Office, is meant to be permanent for the duration of the operation. It should be broken only when thing go badly wrong.

Mair arrives in New Bradwell late in the evening. Built in the nineteenth century by the London, Midland and Scottish Railway company to house its workers, it is a neat village of straight roads and red-brick terraced houses. Possessing only the name and address of her new landlords, she makes her way through the quiet unlit streets. Even at night, recent bomb damage is still visible. A redundant railway track has been mangled by a device and a building in the village blasted by a stray bomb. Why this backwater should have been targeted by the Luftwaffe is unclear but there is one compelling theory. Could it be that word had reached the Third Reich of an important intelligence base buried somewhere in the home counties? That night a stray bomb also fell on the gates leading into Bletchley Park. The Germans had no idea how close they were. There would be no further bombings in the area.

New Bradwell was a smaller version of Bletchley. It was a twenty minute railway journey north and I felt I had reached the end of the earth. On a highly secret assignment, completely alone, I was far removed from cosy Wales and the people I loved. It seemed a peculiar area, this; a few small towns joined together by woods and fields. It was not pretty in a conventional way but not ugly either; just plain

*and nondescript. I saw signs of railway works and brick
factories but no coal mines or steel foundries.*

The area is dominated by the company's railway works in nearby
Wolverton, also built to house LMS's employees. Until 1925 it was
home to the largest steam tram in the world, used to transport
workers and shuttling between Wolverton and Stony Stratford.
It was the last tram operated by steam in the UK but when tram
staff joined the General Strike in1926 the tramline closed and
never reopened. Funded by local businessmen, including at one
time Bletchley Park grandee Sir Herbert Leon, the works had
been taken over by successive railway companies, but even so this
failed wonder is still putting Wolverton and district on the map.

While the Wolverton works were famous for building railway
carriages, and also the home of the Royal Train, the advent of
the war brought about a complete gear change. Since it was a
major manufacturing facility, the works were camouflaged by
painting the outside walls green. Now, instead of manufacturing
railway carriages, its powerful engineering and woodworking
capabilities are used to produce enormous horse gliders, used
to transport paratroopers during the D-Day assaults. They were
also used to carry bombs. The works also repaired other aircraft
and it converted over 700 commercial motor vans into armoured
vehicles too.

Large numbers of children have been evacuated to the area
from London on the basis that this village, fifty miles north of
the capital, is in the "country". As Mair disembarks at the railway
station, she notices recent bomb damage.

*By the time I got to New Bradwell it was getting dark. I
turned into a street of neat and small railway cottages. They*

all looked the same to me, and the absence of light gave everything an eerie feeling. I knocked at the door of my new address and I was greeted by a woman in her late forties wearing an apron. She was plump and had unremarkable looks. There was no real welcome; she didn't smile when she opened the door and she wouldn't for the next six weeks.

"I'm Mrs Hill," she said. "You must be Mare Thomas. (That's how she pronounced my name from then on [rather than My–r]). You'd better come in. Mr Hill is working nights in the Wolverton works so he won't be home tonight."

The terraced house had a long passageway that led from the front door to the scullery, where they lived. The front room, or parlour, was reserved for Sundays or special occasions. I was never allowed in there. The smell and the heat of the coal fire gave an initial impression of cosiness, but how wrong I was.

My new landlady barely said a word to me as she led me upstairs to my bedroom. It was her son's room who was a teacher somewhere in the south of England and recently married. Before she asked anything about my history or family life she started talking about him; how gifted and bright he was and how being a teacher meant he would do well for himself. She considered teaching to be a proper job unlike the wartime work I would be involved in. I was biting my tongue at this point; I wanted her to know I was on top secret government work, much more important to the war effort at that time than teaching. But I said nothing.

My room was plain, with patterned wallpaper, a single bed, a small desk, and a mirror. It had a view of their long garden which had been given over to growing vegetables; row upon row of neat runner beans and garden peas.

Beyond the garden lay another terrace of houses that looked exactly like this one. For the first time that day I had a feeling of familiarity; these houses were like the ones back home.

I sat on my bed surrounded by the silence of the house, a feeling of aloneness creeping over me. I wasn't somebody who got low very often, but I struggled that night.

I went downstairs to the kitchen where Mrs Hill was silently cooking supper – some kind of boiled vegetable broth, as far as I could tell. She gestured to the kettle on the stove and said it had recently boiled and I could make a cup of tea if I wanted. I tried making conversation, but she didn't engage with me. After a few minutes I felt more and more awkward and walked towards the scullery.

I drifted back into the kitchen and tried once again to talk to my new landlady. Our conversation took the form of an interrogation peppered with offensive comments on her part. She'd heard I was from Wales but she had no desire to visit the place. I pressed her on this, wondering why she might have formed such a strong objection to my country. She replied that it was largely peopled by sheep and overridden by hills and coal mines. She had it on good authority that the people who lived there were so backward and poor that they were forced to live in caves.

Forgive me, Lord, but I wanted to punch her in the nose. I'd never come across anyone this ignorant and stupid before. How dare she insult my home like this? She meant it; she wasn't joking!

I pointed out that Wales was completely unlike her caricature. It was a beautiful country full of lovely people – my homeland, of which I was very proud. My parents had ensured I received a very good education and I was a graduate of Cardiff University. I couldn't resist adding that this was probably more than most of the residents of New Bradwell had achieved.

As my voice rose in indignation, she cut across me. The mention of university further provoked her as she rattled through her impassioned viewpoint. Her only son had been to a very good college of course, much better than university. Universities were good for nothing. He had been to a teacher training college in Bedford and came out with a job… He was now teaching in Portsmouth and she was confident he'd be headmaster before he was thirty. Of course he wanted to fight for king and country, but he was told that his job was far too important for that. University was for people who just wanted to talk and were frightened of a hard day's work. Moreover, he had married a lovely girl from Southampton. What a wedding that was!

Then came the knockout blow.

She didn't know what I was doing around here, but the government were paying them to host me. She had said she didn't really want a Welsh person and if she was my mother she wouldn't have let me take other people's jobs when I should be at home working.

I saw red and a huge sense of injustice seemed to pop inside me. I blurted out, "How dare you speak of my parents like that. I'm here to serve my country and fight the enemy, not people like you. My mother died six years ago and she would be so proud of me. I can't believe you've just said that to me."

With that I ran upstairs into my bedroom and howled and howled. I was so upset I stayed up there and didn't eat *the boiled vegetable broth – I wasn't invited to eat the meal and I would have declined anyway. I was furious with this woman and wondered how on earth I was going to stay here for another day, let alone the duration of the war. I went to bed very hungry and sad. Whatever Bletchley Park achieved, could it really be worth this?*

CHAPTER 10

AUGUST 1941 First Day at Bletchley Park

Mair is exhausted after her first night in New Bradwell. Unable to sleep following the confrontation with Mrs Hill, this is not an auspicious start to her new career. The interview with Miss Moore seems far away and her digs and the location she's in bear no resemblance to the grandeur of the British and Foreign Commonwealth office.

The next day at 8 a.m. I walked to a staff bus that would ferry us to Bletchley Park. A large number of people must have had lodgings around New Bradwell for the coach was full with people working various shifts. It was always full, day and night. I know I hadn't slept well the night before, but I felt as though I was in a dream world. I wanted to pinch myself. I wouldn't say that I felt like Cinderella going to the ball or like the sleeping princess being kissed by a handsome prince, but I did feel special. Me, a girl from Pontycymer, about to work for the Foreign Office. I was excited, apprehensive and scared at what was ahead

*of me. I also realized that I didn't have any idea what I
would be doing...*

*As the bus stopped at the ornate gates of Bletchley
Park, I couldn't see the country house in which I would
be based. But as we trod on the crunchy gravel driveway I
saw this strange-looking building sweeping up on our left.
It was imposing and grand, but not as impressive as I had
expected. I had assumed I would see something similar to
the grand mansions I had seen in London, but this looked
quite small and a bit odd. I'm no architect, but this house
looked like it was made up of different parts all somehow
joined together. It was a most peculiar place to look at.*

Bought by London millionaire Sir Herbert Leon in 1883, he
extended the original farmhouse and turned it into a mansion.
Bletchley Park was a country house set in large grounds. Also
known as Sammy, he was a Liberal MP for Buckinghamshire,
High Sheriff of Buckinghamshire and a Justice of the Peace.
As well as holding directorships of international media and
communications companies, he was on the board of the
Wolverton Tram Company. Among his friends he numbered
David Lloyd George, Prime Minister Asquith, the Prince of Wales
and the Duke of York.

Following the deaths of Sir Herbert and his wife, Bletchley
Park became the property of their son, Sir George Leon. He was
disinclined to keep it for himself so it was put up for sale in 1937
and bought by a local businessman, Captain Hubert Faulkner.
Faulkner was a builder and developer and his intention was to
demolish many of the existing buildings and convert the others
into cottages and flats. However, in 1938 Faulkner was approached
by agents representing a branch of the Foreign Office known as

the Government Code and Cypher School. They were looking for a quiet base from which to carry on their duties.

Then comes the stuff of espionage legend. As Prime Minister Chamberlain's misguided attempts to appease Hitler in the 1938 Munich agreement crash and burn, a strange house party begins to meet in BP. It looks like a set of toffs enjoying a relaxed weekend together at a country house; a top London chef from the Savoy Hotel is brought along to perpetuate this piece of misinformation. Known as Captain Ridley's Shooting Party, MI6 staff arrive at BP to oversee building works, erect huts and plan its future operations. And while Captain Ridley sounds like a character fresh out of the pages of P. G. Wodehouse, this group's intentions are entirely real.

Under the operational command of Commander Alastair Denniston, brilliant new appointments follow. These include Frank Birch and Dillwyn "Dilly" Knox. They have been at Cambridge together and both are cryptographers. Additionally Birch has been a West End actor and theatre director, who played the part of Widow Twankey in a 1930 version of Aladdin. Others follow, including Oliver Strachey, Gordon Welchman and the most brilliant of them all, Alan Turing. A Mancunian by birth, Turing has studied at King's College Cambridge and will be credited with being one of the early pioneers of modern computers.

The trawl for greater numbers of recruits continues in earnest in 1939. These bright young things come mainly from the universities of Oxford and Cambridge, mostly mathematicians, linguists and musicians. They will be engaged in decrypting and analyzing Germany's greatest intelligence weapon – the Enigma machine.

Most of the initial intake in 1939 comes from the narrow social networks of Denniston, Knox and Birch. After the onset of war it becomes apparent that a great many more personnel will be required. Thus there is now a concerted effort to make contact with other universities, including Cardiff, to find suitable candidates who can decipher secrets, and keep quiet about it all for decades.

One of Captain Faulkner's unusual legacies to the new owners is a series of huts, built in preparation for the demolition of large parts of the house. They vary in size and some of them already have plasterboard partitions. Most, however, are one-roomed constructions, easily adaptable inside. The Foreign Office sense their potential for housing staff and more of them are added in preparation for the new recruits. Gordon Welchman creates a system which means that each one of the huts has a specific expertise and also a culture of independence. Apart from BP's senior management, none of the employees will have any knowledge of the workings of their colleagues in the other huts. This total lack of information flowing between the numerous huts makes it easier for the authorities at BP to maintain the air of secrecy essential to their work. Careless talk costs lives and could attract unwanted attention to the government's crucial intelligence-gathering operation.

Despite the unflattering grandeur of the main house, the bulk of the code breaking work takes place in these temporary buildings. In addition to existing huts, others spring up like pop-up buildings. In total, fifteen wooden huts are built during the course of the war. Some remain, others are built and taken down, and eventually new brick blocks are built to accommodate the 10,000 staff who eventually work in BP. Their placement is not sequential, thus causing confusion when Hut Three is next door to Hut Six.

When Mair joins the staff, there are six huts in the grounds. Hut Four is nearest the mansion and is dedicated to the Naval

Section. Long after the war is ended and BP becomes a tourist attraction, this hut will summon up the atmosphere of a Second World War NAAFI. Hut Five specializes in Japanese operations and Hut Eight is for the naval Enigma. Huts Three and Six are the hub of the operation; the former deals with general army and air interceptions whereas the latter translates the data received from Hut Three. Hut One houses Alan Turing's pioneering deciphering machine called the bombe. Hut Two is for relaxation.

The hut system, which will become one of BP's most distinctive features, is one of Gordon Welchman's brainwaves. This is how Welchman describes the BP huts:

> … the Bletchley Park huts were single-storey wooden structures of various shapes and sizes. Hut six was about 30 feet wide and 60 feet long. The inside walls and partitions were of plaster board. From a door at one end a central passage, with three small rooms on either side, led to two large rooms at the far end. There were no toilets; staff had to go to another building. The furniture consisted of wooden trestle tables and wooden folding chairs, and the partitions were moved around in response to changing needs. (Gordon Welchman, *The Hut Six Story*, London: Allen Lane & New York: McGraw-Hill, p. 10)

None of the huts are open plan in the modern sense. Each one contains specialized sections, depending on the nature of the work being carried out. For example, Hut Six contains a couple of registration rooms where intercepted messages are brought initially by courier and later by electronic means. There is a decoding room, machine room, control room and a small office where some of BP's most famous cryptographers pore over the decoded messages as they try to work out the settings being used.

Mair's initial impression of the house is not flattering:

BP was a Victorian stately home, and I overheard somebody with a plummy accent describing it as the ugliest country house in the whole of England. Sporting a variety of architectural styles, it left and continues to leave the visitor with a sense of bewilderment. Prior to the war, the house's gardens were apparently rather grand and beautiful. Where the grey huts stood had once been a rose garden, but all this had been sadly demolished.

The people who worked at BP were refreshingly different as well. Even though I had grown up in a small South Wales valley, I considered myself to be cosmopolitan, because of living in London and going to university. But neither of these experiences prepared me for life at BP.

There were a number of other people starting that day; in fact, other buses had also pulled up just outside the gate discharging new recruits, all looking equally unsure of where they were and what they were meant to do next. Having seen the house I imagined we would report there and be given our orders. But no one went that way. I took a few steps to go in, but a man took hold of my coat and said, "No, missy, you don't want to go in there." Not wishing to seem stupid I didn't ask where I should be going to, and I followed the general drifting direction of everyone else.

There were people scurrying around busily, some in uniform, although most were dressed in civilian clothes. This also varied enormously. I saw men in dark suits, but I also saw quite a few in jumpers and even corduroy trousers. The women were on the whole smartly dressed in frocks and jackets, but many of them wore colourful stockings. This turned out to be a real feature of Bletchley Park life, although I never indulged in it myself. Every day witnessed an array of colourful and sometimes gaudy leg adornments, and they served to raise spirits in an intense and generally serious atmosphere.

As we were passing the main house, I noticed the small lake just opposite. There were a few ducks, even swans, and a few people in uniform sitting on the benches in deep conversation. I also saw a series of ugly-looking large sheds. These were the huts. In the middle of the large driveway, there were five or six women with clipboards waiting to greet us, although there was no warmth to their manner, only a cursory good morning and the reading of lists. A woman announced Hut Six and, since my name was included in this register, I followed her to my new professional home. There were four of us starting in Hut Six that day; all women and all graduates from different universities.

The huts were plain-looking. Built to be temporary, they looked out of place in this grand setting; whitewashed and flimsy. As we entered the hut it felt a bit wobbly and the smell of fresh paint was overwhelming. Mind you, even though the conditions were spartan, I thought, "This is wonderful, just wonderful. I'm going to be doing really important, top secret work here." I felt so privileged.

There were no carpets on the floor, just lino, and nothing on the walls. There were a few small rooms leading off the main corridor, and two larger rooms at the end. One of these would be my place of work for the next four years. It was called the machine room, for a very good reason. There were odd-looking machines on every desk in BP. There were rows of desks alongside the walls and a few at the far end of the hut. Even though it was broad daylight, it was poorly lit, probably due to the windows being rather elevated and framed by enormously heavy and dark curtains.

Despite this intense and focused atmosphere, there were also workmen in there, painting and plastering. The partition wall was still being built, so you could still see through into the next room where there were other women working.

There were women at most of the desks in our section, deep in concentration. No one looked up or said hello and the woman who was our guide barely made any reference to them. She then starting talking to our small group, and she had a really stern voice.

"You are all graduates and have been handpicked to join this very special organization. Much has been given to you and much will be expected. I'd like to remind you that you have all signed the Official Secrets Act and this binds you to secrecy for the rest of your days. You are not permitted to talk about your work here to anyone or indeed the purpose of Bletchley Park. The penalties for you could be very grave, and the consequences for the war effort, disastrous. You will be handling very sensitive information about our enemies' operations and you are sworn to absolute secrecy. If you break your secrecy you will be immediately dismissed from your post and you could even face imprisonment. Are you clear about this?"

We nodded compliantly and then she continued in her clipped, well-spoken English.

"You will be working on a machine which is an exact replica of the German Enigma machine. They are designed and used by the Germans to send coded messages to their *officers and troops. The government has listening stations across Britain where these messages are intercepted and brought here several times a day. In this room you will be asked to determine what settings are being used by the Germans and what messages are hidden in the codes. These codes will be brought to you, and you will punch them into the machines so that they can be decoded. Do you understand?"*

We all nodded again, too afraid to ask anything of the dragon addressing us. In all truth, I don't think any of us had the slightest idea what she was talking about.

"This hut works right round the clock and you will be required to work shift patterns. There are three different shifts: eight o'clock in the morning until four in the afternoon; four o'clock in the afternoon until midnight and midnight until nine in the morning. You will be given a half hour meal break which you must take. Hot meals are served in the canteen day and night. There are no toilets in this hut, or indeed in any of the others. There is a toilet block outside and you may use that."

After this short and sharp address we were shown to our desks. There was no time, however, for any negative reflections on her delivery or manner. And anyway, we had been sworn to absolute secrecy. I felt that I wasn't allowed to express any opinion about anything.

The room in which Mair works is identical to all the rooms in all the other huts. The wall and ceilings are generally coated in beige, magnolia and occasionally a dab of racing green. Windows are skirted by enormously heavy blackout curtains and the lighting is generally dim and channelled through fluorescent strips.

Hut Six was generally considered to be the hub of the entire operation, but I realize I'm very biased. It was almost certainly the busiest. German codes destined for air force and army use were intercepted by various listening stations dotted around Great Britain and brought to Hut Six. In the machine room, we keyed in these various codes into our copies of the Enigma machine. The code was fiendishly difficult to crack but we had some brilliant minds at work in other huts who received our deciphered sequences.

At midday, without any signal or communication, the women in Hut Six rise from their seats and head for the canteen. This is one of the larger huts, set out in a predictably regimented way. The kitchen and serving area is at one end and there are tables in rows for the diners. Unlike the surgical atmosphere of these other huts, however, this place has the smell of comfort.

I enjoyed going to the canteen. It was the one time in the day when I felt relaxed, and the food was pretty good too. People used to complain about the quality there, but I found it hot, fresh and filling. There was always a main course and a pudding. And the atmosphere was jolly; there was lots of laughter and banter going around, especially with the military people. There were quite a few navy and air force personnel in BP and they all seemed to know each other, so they were pretty loud around each other. I rather liked hearing them, even though initially it highlighted my own loneliness. They would regularly tease the kitchen staff about the food and make fun of it. I think they did this because it was the only kind of free expression you could get away with in BP. We couldn't talk openly about our work or the war in general so food became a rallying call for all kinds of disaffected opinions. I'm sure people used food language as a euphemism for their other frustrations and concerns!

Her first time in the canteen also exposes Mair to some of BP's ambiguities. With the severe admonition to keep quiet about her work at all times, she hears fellow workers talk openly about the war and also their own work. This takes the form of a conversation at the lunch table.

I was joined at my table by a young Scottish woman called Mary. I had noticed her working in Hut Six. She was very chatty and asked me what I thought of the woman who addressed us that morning. I felt so awkward, I didn't know what to say. As far as I understood it I wasn't allowed to disclose anything about the hut to anyone. Thankfully Mary wasn't a great listener so my dilemma was solved by her constant chatter. "She's a real witch, but you won't see much of her unless you get into trouble. She mainly looks after the typists in the other rooms. Really she's a glorified secretary."

She then went on to tell me about one of the legends of BP.

"Mavis started here last year; she's been here from the beginning. I started at Easter-time. The amazing thing is that Mavis had broken a really important Italian code which not only prevented the bombing of our ships but had resulted in an ambush on the Italian fleet that was planning to attack us. Mavis was so happy that she ran to one of the directors, Dilly Knox, and they were both shrieking with joy. In fact, the whole of the Cottage, the building in which they worked near the main house, made a racket."

This chat only lasted about ten minutes, but I spent most of the time looking around me, wondering if people were listening and if we were going to be told off or worse at any moment. I was really nervous and by the time we got back to the hut I'd convinced myself that this would be my first and last day at BP. But I was wrong. Nothing happened, nobody noticed and we probably hadn't broken any rules. Nevertheless, I decided then that Mary was a liability and that I should try to avoid her whenever possible. I didn't want to be dragged into anything that made me break my oath of secrecy.

CHAPTER 11

AUGUST 1941 Unravelling the Enigma

My desk was the last one at the very end of the room.
Sitting on each desk were the strangest-looking machines
I'd ever seen, cased in a heavy wooden box and looking like
a cross between a gramophone, typewriter and a shop till.
Each machine had three sets of keyboards and a number of
wheels at the top of the furthest keyboard. We were meant
to use these! Next to my machine was a postcard-sized piece
of paper pasted to the desk, giving very basic instructions.
They didn't enlighten me about the workings of the Enigma,
but simply how to turn it on and off and how to input the
codes we would receive. I don't remember these machines
ever being turned off. They were always left on, due to the
shift system.

In all my four years at Bletchley Park, I never
understood how this thing worked. While the brilliant
scientists used their graphs and fancy charts to understand
what was going on, I looked at the flashing symbols and

letters and wondered what on earth I was looking for. We weren't told anything about the progress of the war, of key battles or campaigns; all I knew is that I might stumble on a piece of code that might help our troops.

Mair's first impression of the Enigma machine is not promising.

The closest thing to it was the till in my mother's dress shop in Pontycymer. But even that isn't much of a comparison. This was bulkier, full of keyboards, lights and wires. I hadn't seen anything like it before and the first time I saw it, I had a terrible sense of doom. This was going to be quite beyond me. That box caused me more sleepless nights and frustration that anything else. Those keys and flashing lights; scrambled messages from afar that were life or death to our troops. But how were we to understand this hidden meaning?

It took me a few months to get used to BP's expectations and ways of working. To begin with I was really scared of making a mistake, but I soon realized that there was so much work coming in for us, the emphasis was much more on getting through it rather than perfection. Every shift saw a steady stream of codes being brought to our desks and after a while I developed a rhythm of work, or rather I adapted what I saw the others doing. Before every shift we were given sheets with holes in them; these were meant to be the Enigma settings that were being used that day.

Alongside these sheets we were also told to look out for certain sequences of text buried in the message. These were so important. The brilliant men had twigged that every time the Germans sent a message, they used a crib to introduce it. This might be about the person sending it, or the weather or even the sender's girlfriend. Anyway, they'd worked out that these cribs were often used repeatedly by the senders, probably out of laziness or routine. So if we could find the crib it would expose the Enigma settings. Some people achieved some success and I did once or twice, but to begin with it was monstrously hard.

Looking back on her experience, her voice is still full of frustration and irritation.

One of the Old Testament prophets once had visions of wheels within wheels. That's what the Enigma was to me. You knew that in order to get to the intended meaning or message, you would have to get beyond their clever camouflage and wheel settings. And even though I grew accustomed to its workings, I found it to be the most infuriating piece of equipment.

This is a box that will not give away its secrets easily and it forms a crucial part of Nazi strategy to gain competitive advantage over everyone else.

Germany's stunning brilliance in the initial stages of the war places them head and shoulders above their enemies. It is based on three advantages – air and land-based blitzkrieg, and the excellence of their communications. The sudden, deadly and overwhelming airborne attacks give their opponents little chance to defend themselves, let alone retaliate, and the land-based blitzkrieg acts in the same way. Whole battalions of Panzer tanks are used to overpower the enemy, creating a lethal impact and leaving catastrophe in their wake. Finally, and this is their big idea, electronic cryptography is employed for the first time. Encrypted strategic orders are delivered in real time to German troops, giving information about enemy movements and issuing commands about the next strike. Through their own intelligence gathering and ability to send these messages, the Germans are always on the offensive. In comparison, the Allied troops seem under-resourced and reactive, not proactive.

At the heart of Germany's capacity to move quickly, deploy troops and strike swiftly is the Enigma code system. It is named after the machine of the same name, a Dutch invention patented for commercial use after the First World War. This weird-looking hybrid is an unlikely war winner. But this device is wired and communicates with other Enigma machines across the map of war. No one else has got anything like this.

Behind BP's complex activity is a simple proposition: how to quickly and secretly discover Germany's military operations to the advantage of the British and Allied war effort. Against all the odds, this is achieved, and the mysteries of this box of secrets are broken into under the noses of the enemy.

The Enigma machine is used solely for the purposes of ciphering and deciphering and it is built on technological and mathematical complexity. From the perspective of the operator, the top layer of the machine contains a keyboard consisting of twenty-six letters, set out in the QUERTZY formation of continental typewriters with no keys for punctuation or numbers. Behind it lies a lamp board, again with twenty-six keys corresponding to the same letters on the keyboard. Whenever a key is pressed it lights up a corresponding letter on the lamp board, although not the same letter. A letter K, for example, might illuminate an L or M but never itself and the small circular windows would light up one at a time. This feature provides the code breakers with a tiny chink of hope. This is a vital clue to the working of the Enigma, although the odds are still overwhelmingly against success. If the same keyboard letter is pressed consecutively it will generate a sequence of different letters on the lamp board. But this sequence is not random; it is generated by the people who set the codes. They do this by means of four wheels at the far end of the top surface. These wheels enable a vast number of ciphers, changing the configurations between the letters of the keyboard and the lamp board. With a fixed wheel at either end and a space for three and eventually four rotating wheels, this unit produces a vast sequence of combinations. Each keying can only be repeated after 16,900 instances. And because each message only contains 250 letters, the likelihood of the sequence repeating is minimized dramatically. These wheels are adjusted three or four times by their German operatives every day.

Then, underneath the keyboard is another unit called a *steckerboard* in German, or plug board in English. It has six double sockets corresponding to the keyboard and lamp board and allows the operator to cipher pairs of letters. It is this facility which gives the Germans the ridiculous odds against their codes being broken. With the addition of new electrical plugs and circuits, the Germans believe they have invented an impregnable system. This is the system that the staff at Bletchley Park was committed to breaking. And that strange machine is the key to it all.

In the build-up to the war, as we have seen, Denniston gathered together a group of academics and civil servants to spearhead the process of breaking the inscrutable German codes. In 1939 the first code breakers arrive in BP, about 100 of them in total. Including more women than men, this select team is drawn from a very narrow social and class network. Some are top-flight academics from Oxford and Cambridge universities while the others are drawn from well-connected families. In the language of tabloid newspapers they are boffins and debs, but among this hundred is a small group of ambitious and clever people. Some are still in their twenties; others are well into middle age, veterans of the First World War. These include Dillwyn Knox, Dennis Babbage, Gordon Welchman and Alan Turing. The latter two in particular will develop a mechanical method of decrypting the Enigma code.

Gordon Welchman is in command of Hut Six and has been recruited from Trinity College, Cambridge where he lectured in mathematics. He joins Alan Turing and others in the Cottage initially, although he is later based in nearby Elmers School to pursue his work. His close working relationship with Turing results in the construction of a bombe machine that is quickly able to analyze the vast number of settings used by the Enigma.

He was friendly enough but very involved in his work. When he was in his office in Hut Six you hardly ever saw or heard him. He was a very good manager in that he delegated most of his responsibilities. He had a number of very able women assistants who ran the hut, and believe you me, they were a formidable bunch. They were deeply loyal to Mr Welchman and did his bidding. He was polite and aloof, but they were unafraid of conflict and implementing the rules that were laid down.

Although Mair routinely describes these men as brilliant, she also recognizes that their relationships with each other were stormy.

Above left: Mair, one year old

Above right: Dada, Mama, and Mair, Pontycymer, 1920

Left: Mair (right) and sister Beti in the summer holidays, Borth-y-Gest, 1927

Ffaldau primary school, 1926

Dada, Mair, and Uncle Sam at Porthcawl, 1932

Above: Mair (in the middle) at Aberystwyth, 1934

Left: Mair and Beti in their back garden after the death of their mother, February 1935

Nine delegates at the Baptist Missionary Society summer school, Llandrindod, 1936. Russ is on the left of the front row.

Beti and Mair in the garden of Bryncerdd, Pontycymer, 1937

Mair (left), cousin Bessie, and Beti on a picnic, Porthcawl, 1937

Mount Hermon puddox team, 1937. Vice-captain Mair is on the far right of the front row.

Four Mount Hermon students with college dog, bedroom number 8 circa 1938. Mair is on the right.

Mair at Mount Hermon, 1938

Dada and Mair at the Gower, 1938

Mount Hermon picnic 1938: Mair is the second from the left

Cardiff University: Mair is in the centre on the back row with fellow students, 1939

Mair, Cardiff University, 1941

Russ at the Gower, 1941

Mair and Russ's children in 1961. Helen (top left), Elizabeth (top right), Iwan (bottom left), David (bottom right), and the author, Gethin, who is in the middle held by the girls.

Russ and Mair, 2008

*There were terrible rows and quarrels. I never heard them
going at it, but lots of people had heard them and talked
quite openly about it. None of us knew what they were
arguing about but Dillwyn Knox and Gordon Welchman
really disliked each other. I can't imagine Alan Turing
quarrelling with anyone; I think he would have been
disturbed by his own shadow.*

Luckily for the British and Allied troops, a trio of outstanding
Polish cryptographers, Marian Rejewski, Jerzy Rózycki and
Henryk Zygalski have already started working on decrypting the
Enigma code. The Poles have been developing a machine called
the Bomba, an attempt to mechanically break open the Enigma
by analyzing its rotor settings at speed. Due to a number of
changes introduced by the Germans, the Polish mathematicians
run out of resources to pursue their project and hand their
research over to BP.

*These Polish scientists were legendary in BP. More or less
as soon as I arrived, there was talk about them. None of us
could pronounce their names but we were told that it was
their brilliance and courage that enabled Alan Turing and
his colleagues to crack the Enigma code.*

Turing and Welchman introduce a number of changes to the
now renamed bombe. Of crucial significance is the realization
that each piece of code contains a crib, mentioned above, created
by the Enigma cipher clerks as a kind of short introduction to
their message. It becomes increasingly obvious that many of these
cribs are used repeatedly. Their repetition suggests that once they
have been recognized, the settings for that key can be broken.

The bombe is able to analyze the permutations of each scrambled setting in a matter of minutes.

They were brilliant, utterly brilliant. I was in awe of them, especially Alan Turing. They somehow helped us do the impossible and to this day I have no idea how they or we did it.

The British Tabulating Company based in Letchworth is tasked with manufacturing bombes for use in BP and elsewhere. The company also produces revised versions of its British Typex machine, replicating the settings of the Enigma.

The raw, coded and intercepted German army data makes its way to Hut Six for decoding. The deciphered intelligence is given the name Ultra when passed on to British and Allied military command. The Germans have devised a means of enciphering their messages that is marinated in complexity, and the process of breaking these codes is laborious and sophisticated.

During every shift, intercepted codes would be brought to Hut Six... These codes were sent to the Registry room where they would be booked in before going to a small room where the really bright men worked. They would look at the messages to see if they could identify a crib pattern. If they could, a menu was produced giving clues about which letters were being used to carry the code. These were then passed to our supervisor who in turn tasked us with the job of adjusting our machines to the settings identified in the menu. We had to use the Enigma machine to try to work out what was in it. It was horrendous; I mean, it was full of letters and symbols and thousands of these were coming in every day.

Beyond BP there are a number of listening stations, military and government installations that are intercepting German intelligence. They are called Y stations and run by the army, navy, RAF, Marconi, Foreign Office, MI6 and the General Post Office. These stations combine a mix of direction-finding and interception. Direction-finding tracks the exact location of enemy operation, but it's the intercepted intelligence that is precious to BP. The stations in Chatham and Denmark Hill provide BP with regular and powerful intelligence. Once intercepted and written down, they are transported to BP via motorcycle courier during the early years of the war, and there is a constant stream of couriers coming to BP bringing 3,000 messages daily from all over the country. They are later transported by teleprinter.

Even though the huts are independent of each other in terms of management and staff interaction, they are connected by means of a wooden conveyor belt, carrying these encrypted codes and other communication around BP. When Mair starts works in 1941, it is this rudimentary system that is still in use.

You wouldn't believe the racket it made. It was constantly moving in a clanking, vibrating kind of way. And the noise it made was rather humorous. If you bear in mind that we were all so intense and quiet in our work, this contraption sounded like a big animal that was after our attention. The thing was always groaning, wheezing and shaking; often the flimsy hut would shake along with it. Mind you, it was the only way, I suppose, of ferrying all those messages around the place. Someone told me once that the conveyor machines in BP were based on a similar one found in the big John Lewis store in London. This wouldn't surprise me, as one of the senior managers that came to BP had worked there.

Even though she is a gifted musician and linguist, Mair is at sea with the instructions she is given to place the correct settings on her Enigma machine. Probably due to the extreme needs for security, these settings are never explained to her and neither will she understand the codes she's looking for. Faced with the complexity of the machine, she soon realizes that she is completely out of her depth.

I wasn't a mathematician and neither were the other women I worked with. I had never seen this kind of technology before, and even though it was explained to us several times how it all worked, it all sounded like double Dutch to me. And the atmosphere in our room, in fact in the whole hut, was silent. Sometimes the concentration was so dense you felt you were in treacle. We felt under pressure all the time.

I'd sit there at the start of a shift feeling helpless and inadequate; not emotions with which I was particularly familiar. Until coming to BP I had known quite a lot of success, but Hut Six disorientated me. Believe you me, when you're looking for the unknown using a machine you don't understand, it does nothing for your self-esteem.

I know it sounds terrible and unpatriotic, but the work could be numbingly tedious. The menus were on large sheets of paper and full of lines and letters. We had to look for certain letters and our supervisor knew exactly what we were working on. Once we'd finished our menu, the supervisor rang one of the outstations or huts where the bombes were kept and they would run our deciphered code through those machines. If the code was right, the bombe would stop and the hut informed. A kind of raw joy, a roar of pleasure would

*erupt through the whole hut. It was wonderful and we felt
like we were a real team. It was pure elation, relief and the
noise was deafening, although most of us didn't have the
foggiest as to what was actually happening!*

*I remember overhearing one of the men in the small
room separated from ours by a small hatch, explaining this
very amusingly one day. I don't know who he was talking to,
but it was clear he liked wine from the way he described our
work. He said, "It's as though the Germans have cultivated
a very fine and secret vineyard and are enjoying drinking
the wine every night. They have surrounded their property
with impregnable walls, and for added safety have posted
dozens of armed soldiers on top of each one. But they begin
to realize that some of the wine is disappearing each day,
more and more of it. They can't believe that their security
system has been compromised and so they assume that
some of their own men are stealing the wine. That's what we
are doing. We are stealing their wine with such stealth that
they can only conclude that the problem is internal and not
because of their clumsy enemy."*

This overheard metaphor is accurate. On a number of occasions
during the war, the Germans sense that their movements have
been anticipated by their enemies. This is routinely blamed on
poor security or the presence of spies within Germany. They will
not accept that their codes are capable of being breached. But this
homely picture does address the daunting challenge faced by the
novices in Hut Six.

*To begin with I had no idea what I was doing. And nobody
really explained anything to us. We were just thrown into*

the deep end. There was no training session or lecture,
just basic instructions on what keys to press and then an
attempt to work out the code. After a few weeks, I got the
hang of it, or as much as I was likely to. In the end I thought
of it as a crossword puzzle. I'd always enjoyed The Times
and Telegraph *crosswords, so I tried to approach this task*
in much the same way – except, of course, this was in a
foreign language and all jumbled up.

Also the pressure was so intense that there was no
pleasure in it. The process of keying in these codes was time-
consuming in itself, and then you had to try to decipher it.
Sometimes I would stare and stare at this jumble, trying to
make head or tail of it all. When I started, it still felt quite
small, a few hundred people, but the numbers kept on going
up and up.

Gordon Welchman, in addition to his mathematic genius, also
has a shrewd understanding of the business process and the need
to make BP into a kind of decoding factory.

He was always courteous and good with people, but seemed
to like his own company. Apart from a few men, we were
mainly women in Hut Six. Some of the other huts had more
men but there were an awful lot of girls about the place.
[Welchman] created a process which meant that every
message that came in was broken down and analyzed by
different teams. It could have been so much more confusing
than it actually was. We all knew which area we worked
in, and on the whole that's where we stayed. Some people
moved around in different teams but that was rare.

Other huts have different specializations.

The team in Hut Eight was led by Alan Turing, I think, and also the chess grand master Hugh O'Donnell seeking to break the codes used by the German U-boats and other fleets. This hut had captured an enigma code book from a U-boat – booty that would eventually help unravel the mysteries of the German navy's manoeuvres. This intelligence played a vital part in the tense battles between the U-boats and the Allied convoys.

Mair recalls occasions when someone in Hut Six realized they had broken into that day's code and was sufficiently uninhibited to make it known to everyone else.

A number of people had successfully broken code sequences that led to success in the Battle of the Atlantic in 1941 and 1942. This kind of breakthrough didn't happen very often, but when it did the euphoria we felt was overwhelming. That intense silence was ruptured by the sound of laughter and shouting. It was a hullabaloo! The rush of relief and joy was amazing. All our stiff upper lips dissolved into big smiles. Glee is the word that comes to mind to describe the atmosphere on those rare occasions.

Once an entire piece of code has been successfully decrypted, it is then sent to Hut Three for translation. This hut is populated by linguists, including one of Mair's closest friends.

My friend Dora Sanderson worked in this hut. Even though we had been close friends during my university years, we barely saw each other in BP. And when we did we never spoke about work, which I always thought was highly ironic as she was probably looking at my handiwork most days!

CHAPTER 12

AUGUST–OCTOBER 1941
Is it Over Before it Has Begun?

In these early months, while Mair is learning what is expected of her at BP and feeling more confident in her work, life with the Hills is becoming so unpleasant that her mental and then physical health are severely affected.

Mr Hill was totally different to his wife. Whereas she was curt and rude, he was forever cracking jokes and pulling my leg. Having said all that, he was always rather quiet with her. He was a short, plump man with a ruddy face and pencil moustache. He was a mechanic in the nearby railway works in Wolverton. That was another small town, similar to Bletchley, but dominated by the railways. And he taunted me: "You Taffs might be churning out the coal but we're building the trains that are moving it all around."

Unlike his wife, Mr Hill is greatly interested in Mair's work. But combined with his edgy humour, the impact on Mair is not restful. Mixed in with his relentless jocular teasing is a curiosity about his tenant's mysterious working life. Undeterred by Mair's refusal to say anything other than repeat the "I'm working for the Foreign Office" line, he starts adding a mild threat.

You've got some secrets, and even though you're not going to tell me when you're awake, I bet it will all come out when you're asleep. All those things you do down there in Bletchley will pour out of you when you talk in your sleep. It's all got to come out somewhere. I heard a play on the Home Service about the way they make spies talk, how they deprive them of sleep and force them to spill the beans. I'm going to be outside your bedroom when you sleep to catch whatever it is you have to say.

It may be meant as a joke, but it makes Mair anxious. Already at odds with the woman of the house, she begins to dread bedtime. Even though her intense shifts at BP make her long for sleep and rest, she cannot switch off.

He was so nosy about Bletchley Park. After only a few days of working there, he kept on plying me with questions, trying to trip me up. Who worked there? What did we do? How much did we know about the Germans? Was I a spy? The questions were endless and possibly meant in good humour, but they did make me feel tense. Telling me that he would stand outside my bedroom door at night waiting for me to give some secrets away in my sleep – it really got to me. Ever since I had signed the Official Secrets Act, I was terrified of betraying any confidence whatsoever and

it preyed on my mind. Within only a few days of being in
the Hills's home, I developed a kind of insomnia. I became
anxious about sleep talking and walking into the hands
of the enemy. It was totally ridiculous, but very real at the
time. I had never had issues with sleep talking but this was
the fevered mental atmosphere in which I was now living.

A pattern of insomnia now develops, with Mair fearful of betraying any intelligence she may have come across during her shift. She is now in a permanent state of red alert. Not only can she not relax in Hut Six, she is trying to watch what she is doing, even in her sleep.

Mair never knows if he actually stands outside her bedroom. As a married man in a small house it is unlikely, but the force of the threat is real to her. And what is the subtext of this episode? Menacing words, mild flirtation, invading another's sense of well-being; these are the ingredients of nascent abuse.

Night after night would pass without sleep. It was
particularly bad at night when he was around but I found it
hard to sleep in the daytime; I just couldn't get used to going
to bed when everyone else was getting up.

As the weeks go by, the nocturnal references increase along with the constant attempt to extract morsels of information from Mair.

"What was that you said last night? I'm sure you said
something about Herr Hitler and the Russians in your sleep.
The walls aren't very thick, you know; you need to be more
careful. But I tell you what, why don't you tell me now? It'll
be our little secret."

However, a tense domestic situation is about to be made considerably worse. One morning, as she prepares to catch the bus to BP, Mrs Hill comes to Mair's room with a piece of news. Her daughter-in-law will be visiting them for a few days and Mair will need to move rooms.

Mrs Hill delivered a diktat: "You will need to vacate your bed, Miss Thomas, and we will erect a bed for you in the bathroom. You will be perfectly comfortable and no one will disturb you at night, as other arrangements have been made. However, please do not lock the door, in case of emergencies."

Mr and Mrs Hill's house, like many others in New Bradwell, had an indoor bathroom and toilet, along with an outside toilet. This is due to the foresight of the LMS when the houses were built, at a time when most of the working-class population only had an outside toilet and the bath was a wooden tub in the kitchen. And it is as bad as it sounds. The "bed" consists of a wooden board placed across the bath. There is no mattress, just a bottom sheet that is somehow meant to make it cosy, and an eiderdown and sheet over the top of this precarious sleeping place. Mair's fortunes have worsened dramatically. She no longer has a space of her own, is battling with mental and physical exhaustion, and has to endure Mr Hill's constant jibes.

I felt totally exposed and humiliated when the daughter-in-law arrived. She was just as snooty as Mrs Hill and barely acknowledged me. But my inability to sleep was making me anxious and disorientated. Somehow I managed to concentrate at work, but there were plenty of times when

I could feel myself drifting off in the warm and airless atmosphere of Hut Six. And there was no one I could talk to. I hadn't made any friends yet; the whole culture of BP was against making close friends and talking about anything.

During those few days she was staying, I was working the late shift and arriving back at one in the morning. I was cleaned out from the toil of trying to work out the riddles of the Enigma codes. All I wanted to do was collapse into a warm bed and turn my brain off. I was absolutely exhausted, and all I had to look forward to was a hard board in a poky bathroom. Not only was it uncomfortable, I was also aware that the slightest movement could cause the whole thing to collapse. I'd end up in the tub and wake everyone up.

Even though this period lasts less than a week, time drags. Six weeks have now passed and the inquisitive, ambitious young woman who arrived at New Bradwell station has been replaced by a withdrawn and unwell woman. Constantly tired, full of catarrh and a hacking cough, she shuttles back and forth to BP in her own private world of espionage. But these symptoms deteriorate and she is soon shivering and sweating, clearly ill to all who come across her.

Her relationship with her landlords is virtually non-existent. Mr Hill persists with his caustic teasing; all conversation with Mrs Hill has dried up completely. The combination of chronic sleeplessness, unhappiness and the intensity of the work at BP finally takes its toll. In the spirit of secrecy that is now overshadowing her life, she has told no one about her oppressive experiences in New Bradwell and is internalizing all her frustration and fear. Everything comes to a head during one evening shift.

*I started shivering at work and I couldn't stop.
Maintaining a normal temperature there was virtually
impossible at the best of times because of the damp and
awful heating; but this was different. I broke out into
a damp sweat while also feeling frozen. My teeth were
chattering and my head felt so heavy. I said to myself, "Get
a grip, Mair, you can't afford to show weakness, you're
letting the side down." But it made no difference. I felt
terrible and within a few minutes my body was aching.
None of the other girls noticed; they were all too busy with
their work. After trying to compose myself and not make
a fuss, I started feeling dizzy and in the end I fainted and
slid off my chair onto the floor.*

*I came round in the sickbay, having been taken there
by Mary and a girl called Gillian. The doctor asked me
to open my mouth, shone a little torch into my eyes and
checked my heart rate. "You've got flu, Miss Thomas, and
you're very run down. You're not fit to carry on here, so
for the time being I'm going to sign you off and you're to
go home and rest." His manner was brusque, but his words
felt like pure wisdom. I'm not sure why, but I started
weeping. It wasn't like me to cry. With that, a nurse came
and put her arm around my shoulder. In between my deep
sobs, all my unhappiness about life in New Bradwell came
tumbling out; especially about sleeping in the bathroom,
Mr Hill's menacing sense of humour and my lack of sleep.*

*The doctor and nurse were furious. "We'll see about
that," said the nurse. "I'm going to talk to the main office
now and arrange for you to go back to New Bradwell
immediately and home tomorrow. Is there anyone who
could come and pick you up tomorrow?"*

The only person I really wanted to see was Russ. I explained he was in the South Wales Baptist College, and would they telephone the college and ask them to enable him to meet me in New Bradwell the following day?

Within about half an hour, the nurse returned. Transport had been arranged to take me back to my digs and Russ would come and meet me tomorrow and take me home on the train. I would be given six weeks sick leave at home and, on my return, I would be accommodated in a guest house in Bletchley before finding a more suitable place to stay. I was given pills and medicine and told to get better and not to worry about anything. Arrangements would be made to take my luggage home. "We will be having words with Mr and Mrs Hill," she said. "I don't think they'll be having any more of our people."

The rest of the day was such a blur that I don't remember how Mrs Hill reacted to my sudden return or indeed to the "words" that were spoken to her. But thanks to the medication I was given, I did sleep that night, the best night's sleep I'd had in months.

Mair is exhausted mentally and physically. Sleeplessness has caught up with her, and her immune system is compromised. Russ arrives the following afternoon and the couple return to Wales.

I had come to BP with a sense of destiny and pride, but now I was being forced to return home with broken health. I asked myself disturbing questions about my future prospects there. Could I resign, or ask to be seconded somewhere else? Up to this point, I had succeeded in more or less everything I'd set out to do, but this challenge seemed beyond me. We got on the train back to Bridgend and Dada met us and took us back home by taxi. I had not expected to make this visit until Christmas.

I don't remember the journey at all; I must have slept through most of it, wrapped in a travel rug that Russ had brought me. About a week later, I poured my heart out to him and asked him whether or not I should leave BP. He was adamant I shouldn't and said I shouldn't be intimidated by ignorant people. I didn't share much of this with Dada and nothing at all with my aunties. True to form, they were highly suspicious of my presence in Pontycymer and couldn't resist a few jibes. Aunty Car in particular was patronizing towards me. It was clear she thought I was trying to pull the wool over Dada's eyes about my top secret work, but she was having none of it. She thought I was a foolish young thing with ideas well beyond her station. After six weeks at home, I couldn't wait to get back to BP.

CHAPTER 13

NOVEMBER 1941 St Joan

Mair returns to Bletchley Park towards the middle of October; her health is back to normal and she is generally excited at the prospect of the work facing her.

It was a relief to get back to routine. My visit home seemed to create a strain within the wider family. Apart from Dada, who was always so supportive, I was surrounded by people who had an opinion about me. Most of my aunties and cousins thought the whole "working for the Foreign Office" story was made up. Some of them thought I was deluded while the others saw it as some kind of malingering on my part. But underlying this tension was a more fundamental disagreement. Most of my relatives disagreed with my decision to leave home. They didn't like it when I went to Mount Hermon or Cardiff University and this latest departure was the icing on the cake as far as they were concerned. This had been simmering for years; I should stay at home and look after my widowed father and young sister. And I know that if Dada had even hinted that he wanted me to remain at home I would have done so.

But he wanted me to have a life and I was eager to play my part in the war.

I suppose it's also true that I didn't want the future that Pontycymer had to offer. Compared to London, Cardiff and now BP, it was parochial, limited and I wanted more. If Russ and I were to marry, I realized I would probably not have the material comfort I had known at home, but the adventure of serving God together and having a family eclipsed those minor considerations.

Mair is given new accommodation in Bletchley itself, but only until she is able to find new lodgings. Her temporary billet is only a few minutes' walk away from BP, in one of the adjoining streets. For the time being there are no more buses and exasperating landlords.

The first few days were extremely happy ones. It felt like a new university term and I was so happy to see everyone again. Mary and Gillian, who had been so kind to me when I fainted, were delighted to see me and proceeded to fill me in with all the gossip. I must say that I began to feel uncomfortable with their openness, especially as they talked about Alan Turing's odd behaviour and also told me that quite a few codes had been broken while I was away. Also lots of new people were being recruited every week and I would notice new faces in Hut Six.

I'd only been away for six weeks and it felt as though this strange place had moved on without me. They also said that work had begun on some new blocks to accommodate all the new workers. I told them we weren't allowed to say anything about our work, but they told me not to worry

*so much and take things easy. Everyone shared secrets
and confidences at BP and nothing would happen, even
if you were found out. Thankfully the conversation soon
changed to other things and I was just pleased to have their
friendship. They were different to me in so many ways, but I
appreciated their chirpy and chatty ways.*

A chance meeting in the canteen later that week will alter the
course of Mair's time at BP.

*I was in the lunch queue when I started talking to a girl I'd
seen in Hut Six that morning. Her name was Joan and she
was studying English at Oxford University. This was her
first day in BP and she was trying to take it all in. She was
a pretty, very well-spoken young woman, and it became
apparent that we had a lot in common. Our conversation
flowed freely and the hour lunch break passed like lightning.
Like me she was a Christian and had been part of the IVF
in Oxford; on the committee, in fact. I'd heard about this
group in Oxford and knew that it was much larger than
the one we had in Cardiff. She too was walking out with
someone and hoped that they might get married after the
war. The two of us were also Foreign Office appointees and
shared the same grade as Temporary Assistants. Joan was
part of this new recruitment drive that Mary and Gillian
had told me about.*

*Like everyone else, her initial experience of BP was one
of bewilderment and anxiety. Somehow that morning the
poor thing had succeeded in turning the Enigma machine
off – and this was no mean feat! She had been trying to
find her way around the machine and had located the off*

*button. Much consternation had ensued and she felt really
foolish, although everyone around her was very reassuring.
She thought she might be for the chop even before actually
doing anything, but it wasn't that sort of place. The
managers could be strict about some matters and totally
relaxed on others. None of us were at home with machines
and technology; most people had been academics or come
straight from university. But you never really knew where
the line was drawn and so most of the people lived with a
fairly high degree of fear much of the time.*

*I mentioned to Joan that I'd been ill and had just
returned to BP. I talked about my ordeal in New Bradwell
and I must have been feeling better because I was able to
joke about it now. Joan then suggested that we share digs
together. She was looking for somewhere to stay and hadn't
found anywhere yet. She was staying in another bed and
breakfast somewhere near Bletchley. Her arrival in BP had
been very sudden. Like me she had been approached to
apply for a job with the Foreign Office, had been offered
the post within days and ordered to start her duties
immediately. Joan had been told not to worry about her
studies as she would receive her degree after the war ended.
She had arrived with hardly any clothes and was waiting
for her luggage to be delivered.*

BP holds a list of recommended billets for staff. They are
spread across north Buckinghamshire and into Bedfordshire
and Northamptonshire. But the girls are clear that they want
to be together. They enjoy each other's company and realize
that the intensity of BP might be softened through friendship.
While sharing digs is allowed by BP, they are reminded of their

obligations under the Official Secrets Act. Their determination to live together limits their options, but they approach an address in nearby Newton Longville, just over two miles away from BP.

We didn't have much time to arrange the new digs, but we were both on evening shifts that week so we had a morning to visit the address. A bus took us to Newton Longville and it was a really pretty, old place. The house was a cottage on the main road through the village, and the landlady, Mrs Walters, was lovely as soon as she opened the door. She and her husband had three young boys, and they would be very pleased to put us up. She showed us our room and although not large, it had two single beds and would be big enough for us. We agreed then and there that this would be our new home, and we'd moved in before the weekend.

This relationship will see both women through the war, with little if any conflict, even though they are sharing the same room. This could be due to a common faith or more likely that they will soon be working different shift patterns and hardly together for any length of time. They also discover a common affinity with their new landlords.

Mr and Mrs Walters attended the local church and were very sympathetic to our Christian faith. They even allowed us to hold meetings in their home for BP staff who were Christians. We weren't able to hold them very often because everyone had different shift patterns, but we were successful a few times. Joan and I invited people we knew who had expressed an interest to us, either in Hut Six or in the

> *canteen. We couldn't meet at night because of the blackout,*
> *so we generally gathered in the mornings or afternoons or*
> *in the evenings during spring and summer.*

This return of her religious zeal and general zest in her new friendship is an indication that Mair is now settling into her environment. She is no longer the new girl, and despite her illness she is back on campaigning form. Undaunted by the apparent disinterest of many of their BP colleagues in their gatherings, Mair and Joan manage to create an occasional community of about twenty people who crowd into the small living room in Newton Longville.

> *We had a range of people; some of them were far more*
> *senior than us and a few were considerably more junior.*
> *Most of them were graduates, and we had an equal split*
> *between men and women. One of the men who came was*
> *a mathematician from Cambridge University and very*
> *highly thought of in BP. It was lovely getting to know other*
> *Christians and hearing each other's stories, but also very*
> *limited. We weren't able to discuss our work or any of*
> *the pressures we felt under because we were all under the*
> *Official Secrets Act. So we could only talk and pray in the*
> *most general of terms.*

Mair's converting tendencies are well illustrated by a conversation she had with army officer Maurice Wiles, who attended one of her meetings and would in later years be ordained as an Anglican clergyman and go on to hold the position of Regius Professor of Divinity at Oxford University for twenty-one years.

One lunchtime I met Maurice in the canteen and we had lunch together. I didn't know him particularly well, but he had come to one of our meetings, and after we'd finished eating I suggested we went for a walk around the lake. I could see he was interested in Christianity, but I wasn't sure he was really a Christian. So I tried to encourage him to talk about his faith and whether or not he'd had a conversion experience. He talked in the most vague way, and then told me that his baptism and confirmation had been the most spiritual moments of his life.

I wasn't satisfied by his answer and started telling him that christening and confirmation were all well and good, but that the Bible spoke of baptism being an expression of faith and how could a baby believe anything? I was getting quite heated and annoyed by him. He was very calm and simply said: "Mair, Christians have always disagreed about the sacraments and probably always will. All I know is that God has been pursuing me all my life, particularly on those occasions when I haven't been minded to seek him. I admire your certainty, but I'm finding it harder and harder to reconcile the monstrosities of war with the blinkered naivety of evangelical church people. I don't wish to fall out with you, Mair, and I suggest we both go back to work."

With that he turned and went back to his hut and I stood looking at the lake. I suppose I felt I'd pushed him too far and been rather superior in my manner. Worst of all, he never came again to our meetings and I felt considerable sorrow that I might have been the cause of his disillusionment with us. However, this soon wore off as I was too busy with other matters, and we saw considerable encouragement with the other members in our group.

Oddly enough, not long after my difficult conversation with Maurice, I had a much better chat with a young typist called Jennifer. She didn't work in Hut Six, but somehow or another she found out about our group and that I was one of the leaders. She lived near Bletchley with her father, but was deeply unhappy with her life. She had just broken off an engagement with her longstanding fiancé, who worked in the Wolverton works, and her father was furious. Her mother had died of cancer a few years before and her father wanted her to settle down and marry, but BP had opened her eyes to new horizons and new people. She said she wanted more from life, but she also wanted something deeper; she wanted to know God personally. I felt in my element. I was able to share my experience of losing my own mother at a young age and how becoming a Christian had given me such hope and drive. She listened intently and I asked her if she'd like to become a Christian. She said she'd think about it.

But it isn't all religion and earnest prayer during her free time.

We had work most of the time and there were rarely days off. We were all meant to have time off work, and occasionally we took it, but the work ethic in BP was so strong we generally worked through. And very often you'd be called in anyway… There were so many people off sick all the time that the huts were always short-staffed. This was certainly true of Hut Six.

We had fun as well. A lot of the people in BP enjoyed cycling, and the country lanes around Bletchley were often full of BP people on bicycles. I've never been able to ride a bike, sadly; something to do with my lack of balance and coordination, I think. But Joan and I played tennis quite a lot and in lighter evenings you could always join in with a game of rounders. This was the most popular pastime in BP, and it was a great way of getting to know people and running off some steam.

Best of all, though, was the croquet lawn. I hadn't played croquet since my Mount Hermon days, but I did play once or twice in BP. What was lovely about these games in BP was that they were all inclusive. Anyone could join in and it didn't matter whether you were male or female. I joined a game that was just about to begin, and it was largely made up of men. As I picked up my croquet stick I overheard a rather posh RAF officer, pretty high up I think, speaking to his friends: "What's that Welsh girl doing playing such a civilized game?" This infuriated me and I waited until I could introduce him to my Celtic incivility. After a few hoops, towards the end of the game, I eyed him up and walloped him off the lawn. You should have seen his face! I went on to win.

This episode highlights again many of Mair's most prominent characteristics. When convinced of the rightness of her cause, she loses no time in trying to persuade others to join her. And there have been many causes; getting a good education and preferably a degree has been a dominant theme, and she wastes no time in telling young women in particular to stop wasting their time and go to university; or the need to learn a musical instrument in order to live a more refined life. But none of these issues have been as enduring or as potent as her Christian faith. She possesses an unusual ability to promote her faith in a clear and direct way, without being unduly bothered by the response of her hearers.

CHAPTER 14

1941–42 Loved and Chosen

The end of 1941 and early weeks of 1942 witness some of the war's most memorable events. On the morning of 7 December 1941, Japanese aircraft carry out two overwhelming attacks on the US Pacific Fleet in Pearl Harbor. The fleet has been moved to Hawaii and a military build-up is planned for the Philippines. Up to this point, the Americans have viewed the conflict as Europe's war, but this event changes everything. Five American battleships and 188 of their planes are destroyed, and thousands of personnel are killed. Within twenty-four hours, Japan launches attacks against Malaya, Hong Kong, Guam, the Philippines, Wake Island and Midway Island. The following day, President Roosevelt declares war and describes 7 December as a "date which will live in infamy". This is now a world war. Despite the savagery of the attack and the loss of life sustained, many commentators on the side of the Allies are pleased that the sleeping giant has now entered the war.

When I heard the news I felt relieved. None of us in BP could understand why the Americans had been so slow in getting involved. It felt like we were taking on the might

of the German Axis on our own, and this was now a very
important turnaround. And as it was coming close to
Christmas, there was definitely a new optimism in the air.
I even heard some singing coming from the bar area at that
time; people must have been happy!

However, midway through February 1942, Churchill and his Allies suffer a humiliating defeat at the hands of the Japanese. After nine days of intense fighting in Singapore, the prime minister instructs General Wavell that the battle must be fought to the bitter end and defeat must be avoided at all costs. The honour of the British Empire is at stake. On paper there is hardly a contest. Compared to General Tamoyuki Yamashita's fighting force of 30,000, the British Commonwealth troops number more than 80,000.

On 8 February, Japanese troops land in the north-west of the island and make steady progress, despite the stern resistance of the Australian troops. As the Japanese bomber aircraft enter the fray, their stealth and carefully targeted attacks prove too much for the ponderous defence on the island. Singapore surrenders to the Japanese on 15 February, and this becomes the largest collapse of a military campaign in British history. This event is a further blow to Churchill's attempts to turn the war in favour of the Allies and creates public anxiety that this is a war that cannot be won.

The mood is grim again in Hut Six. The light at the end of the tunnel heralded by Pearl Harbor has been snuffed out by this widely reported calamity. Added to this is the sense that the Battle of the Atlantic is now a grinding war of attrition, with the German U-boats in the ascendancy. This six-year battle will be the longest unbroken theatre of conflict in the whole war. And 1942 is particularly bad for the Allies. Seven million tons of merchant shipping is sunk, and in July alone 143 ships are sunk, followed in

November by a further 117. The sinking of the *Bismarck* in May 1941, largely fuelled by BP intelligence, is a far-off memory and there is real anxiety that the U-boats will succeed in snapping Britain's food chain.

For all the work we were doing and the immense buzz that was being created by Alan Turing's bombe, nothing seemed to be changing. And yet again, the atmosphere of secrecy meant that even if there were successes, they weren't being widely shared. Unless you happened to be in a hut when news came through of success, you'd never hear. And when you did, it was bitter-sweet. I remember once hearing about a piece of code we'd broken which meant that instead of a British loss, we'd been able to sink a German ship. We all cheered, but deep down I thought, "We've just sent hundreds of fathers and sons to their graves. There will be families in grief now because of us." Of course, I never shared any of this with anyone.

It was hard not to talk about all these things, but you just couldn't. And nobody would have listened anyway because we were all frightened of the consequences. But a few people risked it and tried to draw others into sharing their opinions. I noticed this tendency after Pearl Harbor to some extent, and definitely after the fall of Singapore, and the relentless Battle of the Atlantic. We'd hear about a terrible attack with thousands of lives lost and think, "Why couldn't we have stopped it?" We had all this technology and expertise; we had a hut that specialized in the Japanese version of Enigma, for goodness' sake, but we still couldn't stop it happening. Most of us didn't say anything, but there were some who just couldn't stop themselves.

In our hut it was always Mary and Gillian. Mary came from Glasgow and had studied at Edinburgh University before coming to BP. Gillian was from Warwick and had been at Cambridge prior to her work in Hut Six. Both of them were really bright, but not especially political; they just liked to talk about everything and wanted to be in the know. At the start of one evening shift, Mary offered an opinion about the recent crisis in Singapore.

"I don't understand how we're missing some of the plans. I mean, that's all we do in BP, intercept enemy tactics, and we spend all our time trying to crack their codes. And sometimes we succeed, but it still isn't stopping the slaughter of thousands of lives. Why in the end are we doing all of this?" Nobody answered; we all pretended to be getting on with our work.

But Gillian took up the challenge.

"And another thing, all they're doing in the new Hut Seven is decoding Japanese code. You'd think they might be better at it, wouldn't you? We've just lost thousands of men in Singapore when we should have been victorious and Hut Seven didn't see it coming." She was clearly speaking out of turn and very unfairly, but still no one rose to it. Before she could expand on her ignorance, Mr Welchman's assistant came in. She also acted as office manager. I assume she hadn't heard anything because all she said was, "Ladies, here are your settings for this shift," and she proceeded to hand out our first tasks.

How she didn't hear their conversation, I do not know. But these two girls were becoming a liability to the rest of us

*on the shift, and I always seemed to be on the same rosters
as them. They were good fun and not malicious, but they
were inquisitive and wanted to talk about current affairs
and the progress of the war. But I felt I had to say something
to Mary about it all as I was beginning to get nervous
around them.*

*At lunchtime I had a word with Mary and shared my
concerns about the earlier conversation and the Official
Secrets Act. She laughed and said that we were free to talk
about BP in Hut Six and even on the rest of the premises.
I disagreed with her and said we had been expressly
forbidden to talk about our work with anyone. She told
me not to be so silly and that the Act covered disclosing
secrets beyond our circle of colleagues. There was no
persuading her, but I resolved that I wouldn't engage in any
conversation with either of them after that. I realized that
this might make things a little awkward, but I didn't want
to be tarred with the same brush.*

Since her Mount Hermon days Mair has retained an interest in the
fortune of European Jews, but very little is reported in the media.
Neither does the stifling secrecy of BP encourage such inquiries,
but a surprising encounter in May rekindles her interest.

*I was working the late night shifts – by far the worst of all.
Not only were the hours long and quiet, but trying to sleep
in the daytime was also an impossibility; I think everyone
felt the same. I never met anyone in BP who managed the
knack of sleeping properly in waking hours.*

*But you had to take a lunch break, even though it was
3 a.m.! Eating a hot meal at that time of day played havoc*

with my body clock and metabolism, but on the other hand it did break the intensity of the shift. There was no variation in the food offered at night; no light salad or snacks. It was generally some kind of stodgy pie followed by an equally filling pudding. I'm not sure why, but it was always harder digesting food at that time, and you generally felt bloated and uncomfortable for hours afterwards.

One night I sat on the same table as someone called Hyman who came from Sunderland. He was a short man, shy but with piercing dark eyes. I remarked that his name sounded Hebrew and he said he was Jewish. His grandfather was a rabbi and he attended synagogue whenever he could. Although he was new to BP he had already found out that a new synagogue had opened in Bletchley and intended visiting.

I asked him lots of questions but he was reluctant to talk, as though he was suspicious of my motives. However, I found out that he was fluent in the Hebrew of the Scriptures and was thinking about becoming a rabbi himself after the war. I told him of my experiences of meeting Jews in the East End and this seemed to put him at his ease. We talked about the extreme conditions the Jews had been facing in the build-up to the war, and he suggested that things were now a lot worse for the Jews in Germany and Poland. I asked him to elaborate, but he wouldn't and added that these were matters he'd heard his family talk about. All he would say was that the full story would come out eventually.

Despite my experiences of knowing many Jewish people when I was in London, I never once attended a synagogue. I asked Hyman if I could attend the one in Bletchley, but he was uncertain. Some of them apparently allowed Gentiles *to attend and others didn't. Being a Gentile and a woman probably wouldn't help my cause! But it was something I wanted to do and I spoke to Joan about it the following day. She was equally interested and suggested we went along on the next Saturday we both had off.*

The synagogue was on the high street; not a building I had noticed before. We had put on our best frocks and coats and, of course, our hats. Neither of us really knew what we were doing; it just seemed like an interesting way to spend a very rare day off together. By the time we arrived at the synagogue, we were giggling hysterically. Ahead of us we could see a number of men in long black coats and wearing kippahs on their heads.

As we approached the front door, I think we both realized we'd made a mistake. We were unprepared, uninvited and not at all Jewish. We didn't even know whether or not they allowed Gentiles in. Worst of all, we were laughing uncontrollably. Our nerves had got the better of us and we were clinging to each other as we made our way up the steps. Even though disrespect was the last thing on our minds, this is probably what was communicated to the black-suited gentleman who greeted us.

We bolted. We ran down the street until we found a tea shop and fled into it. It was quite full and I noticed a number of other BP people in there. What they must have thought of the pair of us, I do not know. Dressed up to the nines and laughing irrationally; they must have thought we were mad. After a while, fortified by a strong pot of tea, we calmed down and tried to understand our nervous laughter. We were both disappointed with the outcome but realized we had probably been rather naive.

*But Joan was always great fun and that's what was
lovely about our friendship. We shared the same convictions
about many things, but we also laughed a great deal as well.*

In the summer of 1942, Russ is serving a three-month summer
placement in the East End of London. As part of his training as
a Baptist minister he is sent to gain experience by working in the
Shoreditch Tabernacle, a large church numbering over a thousand
adults and children. Next door to its main building, this church
also has a children's church. Unexpectedly, Mair and Joan are given
weekend leave during this period and visit Russ in Shoreditch.

*Russ had arranged for us to stay with an elderly couple who
were members of the church, and they were wonderful.
It meant that Russ and I couldn't be as close as we might
have liked, but that was the way of things then. We were
also both aware of Russ's reputation as a minister and we
didn't want people to get the wrong impression about our
relationship. Even then a lot of people would have thought
our approach was old-fashioned, but we didn't want there
to be even a hint that we were behaving like a married
couple before we actually were. Back in BP I was aware
that lots of people were having flings and affairs and I didn't
want Russ and I to be spoken of in the same way.*

*I hadn't been back to the East End for this length of visit
properly since my Mount Hermon days and I was shocked
to see the effects of the Blitz. There were huge gouges and
scars on the landscapes; broken glass, twisted metal and
rubble wherever you looked. The authorities were trying
to contain the damage and make way for pedestrians and
buses, but it was a mess. But of course, there was a war on*

and so trying to clear up the debris and fight the enemy
could not be done at the same time.

The church was on the Hackney Road and I realized
again how much I had enjoyed spending time in this area.
There were so many nationalities, especially Bengalis and
Jews. Russ was enjoying himself, but this was clearly a
challenging environment for him. I don't think he'd met
many non-white people before coming to Shoreditch, and
here there were probably as many people from overseas
as there were from Britain. Even though South Wales at
the time had many Italians running cafés and men from
Brittany selling onions from their bikes (we called them
Sioni Winwns in Welsh), it was very uncommon to see
people of other colour. But Russ was well suited to this
ministry and the people clearly liked him. He was very easy
around people and took them as he found them. I loved
that side of his character; no judgment or superiority, but a
desire to reach out to everyone he met.

He went for a haircut on the day we arrived and this
made a great impression on him. The barber's shop was
just opposite the church and he said the outside reminded
him of the one he visited in Gorseinon. But that's where the
similarity ended. Inside, the only language being spoken
was Yiddish and the place was packed full of Jewish émigrés
from all over the world.

When it came to Russ's turn, he said he nearly ran
out with embarrassment as he feared he wouldn't be able
to communicate with the barber. But he persevered and
enjoyed the experience of a haircut, wet shave and hot
towels being applied to his face. Thankfully the barber spoke
quite good English and they enjoyed a good chat.

The barber said that Jews were still pouring into the East End and also places like Manchester and Leeds. They were fleeing persecution and the community was very frightened for its future. He repeated something I'd heard from other sources; that the Nazis' aim was to obliterate the Jews altogether. He felt that no one wanted to hear this, but most Jews believed it was only a matter of time when everything would come to light. Russ pressed him on this, but the barber only repeated that more and more Jews were being driven out of their jobs, businesses and homes across Europe; he couldn't understand this hatred of his own people; they were hard-working and inoffensive. They had no armies, no country to defend and no flag to which they rallied. He told Russ that his people were now tired of being the chosen people and that it was high time that God chose another group to pick on. Russ remained silent and for the first time in his life felt the pain of this hated minority.

Sunday was church day; services in the morning, afternoon and evening. Joan and I, however, misbehaved and Russ was cross with us. We walked to the church in the morning and immediately saw that next door was a large building belonging to the church. They called it their schoolroom and there were hundreds of children going into their own church meeting. We popped our heads around the door and were amazed. The congregation was entirely made up of children, all dressed very smartly. Even more striking was the mix of colours and cultures. There were Asian, African and white European children, and very few adults. The pianist was a girl of about thirteen and the boy leading the service and preaching can't have been more than fifteen. I'd never seen anything like it in my life.

It was very moving, but also strange, with all of them behaving like little adults. It was very powerful, but I also found it funny. We both did and started giggling. We couldn't stop and when we tried, one of us would start laughing again. We held each other tightly by the arm and went outside. People were streaming into the church, again hundreds of them. We weren't really in the most reverent frame of mind by now. It was probably a nervous reaction to being away from the quietness of BP and back in normal life, but we simply couldn't control or stifle our laughter.

We stood near the railings leading to the church for a few minutes and I could see Russ was irritated, especially as people were saying good morning to him and then looking at us.

"What on earth's going on, Mair?" he said to me. I was breathing hard by now and trying to get a grip, even though my eyes were watering and Joan was still chuckling.

At that moment a couple of old gentlemen passed us and one of them said to Russ, "That's your sweetheart, isn't it?" Well, that put the tin hat on it, as they would say. Russ went as red as a beetroot and I started giggling again. It was terrible. Russ marched off elegantly, trying to look as though nothing had happened. We followed him into the church eventually, sat near the back and behaved ourselves. Russ preached well and I was proud of him in the pulpit, even though I had embarrassed him with my giggles. We made up at the end of the service, and Joan and I apologized to Russ. He was fine about it; he was never a man to hold a grudge.

From October onwards Mair feels that the shifts are becoming longer and more intense. The workload, already heavy, is reaching torrent level; a reflection of the success of the Y stations in intercepting German messages and the increasing ability of BP to decode them. In North Africa, Rommel's plans to open a route from Cairo to Alexandria and thereafter to secure the Suez canal are constantly being thwarted by broken Enigma intelligence. Eventually he withdraws his troops in defeat.

In November, Mair joins her landlords around the family wireless. It is nearly midnight.

Joan was working but I was at home. Mr and Mrs Walters were very excited and said there was going to be a special broadcast on the Home Service. The prime minister was going to say something. And they were right, because late into the night a special news flash reported Mr Churchill's words. He talked about the way the Germans had been beaten in North Africa and were now in full retreat. He said that this wasn't the beginning of the end, but maybe the end of the beginning. These were stirring words of wisdom and the three of us felt that this was the best bit of news we had heard in years.

Mair returns home for Christmas, although she is given the option to stay on in BP. Generous overtime rates are to be paid and the festive social life will be lively. However, she declines the opportunity.

It just didn't appeal to me. I wanted to see my family and have a break. I'd never been a girl for parties and I didn't like the culture of drinking and smoking I saw all around me. Most of these people didn't share my faith or values, and quite honestly people's morals were very loose; men

*and women swapping partners all the time, it seemed to
me. Quite a number of the men were married, but this
didn't stop them from forming secret relationships. I've often
thought that this was one of the dark sides of BP. The oath
to secrecy which we'd all sworn meant that some people took
advantage and cheated on those people who trusted them
away from BP. It would be a relief to be away from it.*

*Hut Six was also a smoky environment; there was
always somebody puffing on a cigarette or pipe and I
wasn't used to it. Dada didn't smoke and I was fed up with
my clothes constantly smelling of old tobacco. I felt I was
constantly battling with chest infections, and the smoky
atmosphere didn't help me at all.*

Mair's return to Pontycymer, however, is not as relaxing as she
hopes. On the evening of Boxing Day, Mair's aunts descend on
Dada's house. The strained relationship between Mair and her
extended family has not improved with her absence and the year
draws to a close with further conflict.

*All my father's sisters were nosy and constantly asking me
questions about BP. I called them the "Cartref" lot, for
that was the name of the house they all lived in. Aunty Luc
(short for Lucy) was persistent in her questioning, but I
wouldn't budge. And the more I refused to be drawn, the
more irritable she became. She even thought I was being
disloyal to my own family by not trusting them. I explained
time after time that I had signed the Official Secrets Act and
I was unable to say anything.*

*Then to top it off, her youngest son Edward got
involved. He was a pompous, unlikeable young man*

who thought very highly of himself and extremely little of everyone else; everyone except his mother, that is. He turned on me, even accusing me of lying. I knew that he was working as a clerk somewhere in the War Office and he gave the impression of being Mr Churchill's personal adviser. He told me he knew about the secret war effort and that this was all being carried out by the Foreign Office and MI5. He proceeded then to name a few people and the kind of work they were doing. With every word he seemed to inflate with pride, as though talking about his own heroism. He said there were no other departments and I should stop pretending to be so important.

I'm afraid I lost my rag with him that night. I told him that there was far more going on with the intelligence services than he knew about, and that I knew he held a very minor post in the civil service. I asked him directly if he'd signed the Official Secrets Act and his answer was flustered. I told him bluntly that if he had, he was already in breach of it and could face the most awful consequences. If he hadn't signed the Act, then it meant that his rank was so lowly that there were no secrets to keep.

I knew I'd gone too far, but I'm glad I got it off my chest. I did apologize to him later that evening and again after the war ended. As far as I was concerned, we had made up and were reconciled.

On New Year's Day 1942, Russ and Mair enjoy a day out in Swansea. It's a bitterly cold day with a sharp wind and snow in the air. Russ has taken Mair to his favourite spot on earth, Swansea Bay. He likens this place to the Bay of Napoli, which he has never visited.

We'd had a lovely lunch in an Italian café near the Mumbles, but then we walked down to the beach. I could tell he was nervous and there we were, standing on the beach, with a sea gale blowing in our faces, making small talk. All of a sudden, he dropped to one knee and I burst out laughing. He looked so funny kneeling on the wet sand and looking slightly off balance. But he remained serious, took a box out of pocket and opened it. It contained a ring.

"Mair, will you do me the honour of becoming my wife? I love you and believe you are the right one for me." He didn't move; indeed, he didn't say any more than that. I was overwhelmed with joy and relief and I immediately said yes; there was no hesitation or doubt. I knew that Thomas John Russell-Jones was the one for me and I'd known it for years. He stood and we embraced, on the wet sand and in the cold air of Swansea.

He told me that he'd asked Dada the day before, and my father had given his unreserved blessing. He had also told Russ that he knew he wasn't materialistic but Russ needed to know that when Dada died, I would inherit the little terraced cottage he owned across the road. That would be my inheritance and it would be a help to me and Russ and hopefully any children we had.

Russ then prayed, and this was so typical of the man. He wasn't pious or sanctimonious, but prayer was part of his life. He thanked "our loving heavenly father" for love and for me in particular. He prayed that our marriage would be blessed and happy. He even prayed for our children, and I can remember smiling at this – it seemed so wildly optimistic. He prayed God's blessing on them.

He then said to me that he would never be wealthy and his vocation was to serve Christ and his church to the end of his life. I replied that I didn't care where we lived, as long as we were together. I realized that this calling had to come before everything else and we would stand together in this cause.

I didn't tell Russ everything, and not once did I talk about the boffins who worked at BP, or about the various machines I'd seen or heard about, but I felt I needed to share some of it with him. From early on in our relationship, I had wondered if we would be man and wife and I trusted him implicitly. He made me feel safe, and when we were together I felt we were equal partners in our faith and life.

He was very good and he told no one about any of it. This must have been hard for him, especially when all the secrets started coming out in the 1970s and 80s, particularly when even members of my own family chose later on to publicly ridicule my account of working in BP. They more or less accused me of lying about it all, but Russ said nothing. He could easily have dismissed their foolish chatter, but he chose not to and this was the right thing to do.

Having colluded over this secrecy, Russ and Mair will carry this unofficial secret into their old age. This foundation of mutual trust will be built upon and expanded, beyond marriage and family life. A precious and glowing value emerges: nearest and dearest can be trusted with confidences, but be wary of strangers. The world, including the church, is fickle, so trust only flesh and blood. Friends can only be trusted up to a point, whereas the ties of family are strong and sacred. The BP secret, however, even transcends that value and remains the property of these two alone.

This newly engaged couple leave the empty beauty of Swansea Bay happy in their love and aware that no date can be set until and whenever the war comes to an end.

CHAPTER 15

1942-43 Girls Talk

Mair returns to BP in the bloom of love. Once the war ends, she now knows who she'll be with and what they'll be doing. This is now an affair of the heart and she wears her ring proudly.

Beyond her small premarital world, however, the victory of the Allied troops at El Alamein is a shot in the arm for a war-weary public. For the first time since war was declared in 1939, the Axis troops are on the back foot and the Allies are marching forward. BP, however, exists in a vacuum. Except for the few senior managers and officers who are in contact with the various command operations, most of the staff are completely in the dark about the impact of their work. Mair's romantic feelings for Russ and her sisterly relationship with Joan now dominate her personal life. Even though Dora Sanderson was instrumental in Mair's successful recruitment at BP, they haven't spoken properly for years. As with Joan, Mair has much in common with Dora. They share a common faith; both are graduates and both come from Wales. But none of this is strong enough to forge a new kind ·of friendship. Due to her different shift patterns, Dora is unable to attend Mair and Joan's meetings. In March, however, their paths cross again.

I went for a walk along the canal in Fenny Stratford. It was a beautiful day. I felt like getting some fresh air before my shift and I took an earlier bus to Bletchley. I was in my own world when I saw Dora walking towards me on the towpath. We were delighted to see each other again; I'd forgotten how much I had loved her company in the old days – only three years ago, but they felt like another lifetime.

We talked about university days and the IVF, but somehow the same spark wasn't there. She looked tired, with shadows under her eyes and generally sad. I was concerned and began asking a few questions. She said she couldn't stop as she was in a hurry so we agreed to meet up after our evening shift. The canteen would be open; we could have a cup of tea and still be in time to catch the last bus home. This was more of an issue for me as Dora's digs were close to BP.

That night we met in the very dim light of the canteen. It was never a great place at night; the heavy curtains were pulled together and only the most watery of light was permitted. It always felt rather ghostly. We drank our tea and Dora was very silent. She really wasn't the same girl who was so alive and positive when she suggested I apply for BP.

It turned out that her mother was seriously ill and unlikely to live for much longer. She didn't mention her father and I had the impression that he had died in the war. As she spoke of her mother, with great affection, tears began to fall down her cheeks. The lighting was so poor in the canteen that no one would have noticed anyway. She didn't know what to do. She felt she should go back to Cardiff and be with her mother but, on the other hand, she felt a great sense of duty to BP, and especially her colleagues. "It's so hard in there," she said, "and the pressure to make sense of all of this…" Her voice trailed away into the thin yellow atmosphere. We both knew that she wanted to talk about the unending weight of work, but that we were completely unable to support each other.

I had seen this deterioration in a number of other colleagues. The flow of work was constant and the secrecy of the place was oppressive. People went off sick all the time, and I suspect that much of this was due to stress. But Dora and I were bound by the wretched Official Secrets Act and we dare not cross that red line. I tried talking about her options, but in truth she was in her own world. Her dilemma was compounded by overwork and exhaustion. I knew that feeling and spoke about my experience in New Bradwell. She smiled and nodded, but her mind was far away.

She didn't want to prolong the conversation and eventually she told me that unless I was careful I'd miss the last bus home. I looked at the clock on the wall and could see that I only had a few minutes to catch it. We said our goodbyes, agreed that we must meet again soon and I dashed. But I was too late; I had missed the last bus. I could go back to Dora and ask if I could go to her digs, but this wouldn't be fair on my landlords, who might worry. And anyway it was only two miles or so to Newton Longville. If I walked briskly I could be there in less than an hour, I said to myself.

I hadn't bargained on the darkness being so very dark. There were no street lights; in fact, there was no light whatsoever. Walking through the town wasn't so bad; there were a few people about and the houses and streets were familiar, even at night. But when I was out of Bletchley, the night and the silence heaped up on me. The road to Newton

Longville took me out into the countryside, and up to this point I'd only seen it from the inside of a bus. This was different. I could hardly see where I was going; no traffic, no landmarks, only the big trees silhouetted against the black sky. I trudged along the road, hoping I was going in the right direction.

After about a mile or so, aware only of the sound of my breath and the cry of owls, I was convinced I could hear another noise. My pace quickened, as did my pulse. But the noise disappeared and it was me again with the sound of breathing. It was a cold, clear night and my eyes were now acclimatized to the different shades of dark. Then I heard it again, behind me – the sound of footsteps. They were in time with my own, but definitely were not an echo of mine; softly, softly then a heavier thud, thud. I panicked, breaking out in sweat. I was still a long way from home. There were constant rumours of dangerous people at large in the countryside; escaped prisoners of war from the nearby camp, or German spies parachuting down in the darkness.

So I started walking very quickly and then gently running. Surely he wouldn't keep up with me. I turned round and peered into the night. I was sure I saw the figure of a man who seemed to be going at my pace. I just ran as fast as I could. I bolted down the street. Thank God! Houses, cottages, not Newton Longville but life and civilization. I had a sudden idea. I recognized these houses. They looked the same as the one I lived in; that meant they would have outside toilets. I ran through an open gate into a toilet and bolted the door behind me.

I stood there in the pitch dark, panting, trying to stifle my breath, heart pounding against my ribs. Was he outside?

*Would he smash the door down and attack me? All I
could hear was the wind rustling and a dog barking in the
distance. I waited as the seconds became minutes, until
more than an hour had passed. I had to get home. Surely
there was no one out there. I summoned my courage and
ran and ran down the lane. He'd have to move quickly to
catch me now. I was running blindly down a winding road
and my foot caught a drain cover. I fell headlong, my body
crashing and scraping against the rough surface. I yelped
in pain; I was trapped. I lay there expecting to meet my
pursuant. But nobody came and nothing happened. I rose
and hobbled back to my digs, now only a few hundred yards
away. Thankfully my landlords were in bed and were none
the wiser about my little adventure.*

This strange episode illustrates the constant fear Mair feels that she is being watched; that her secret life is fragile and might be exposed in some brutal way. It is probably a universal experience for people working in BP. The pressure for complete confidentiality, long working hours and poor ventilation in the huts might explain the high levels of sickness. Employees are regularly away from work with chest conditions, flu and exhaustion. Mair's best friend, Joan, succumbs to flu in April and returns to her Oxford home.

Happily for Mair, she receives a letter from Russ informing her that he's coming to see her. Even though he's tied up with college and church work for much of the Easter holidays, he has a few days' leave and is looking forward greatly to being with her again.

*My stomach churned when I read his letter. I wanted to
see him and there were so many things I wanted to tell him
about BP; except, of course, I couldn't. But I also wanted to*

start planning our wedding day, even though we couldn't do much until this war was over.

The days before his visit seemed to drag. But then the day came, and after my shift there he was, waiting for me, sitting on a bench outside the main gates to Bletchley Park. He had no idea what I was doing in there – neither did I for much of the time. He always looked smart and he was no different then, sporting a grey suit and blue tie. I wanted to hug him, but instead we shook hands warmly and immediately started talking. We talked and talked about university, about the IVF, our families, Russ's work and nothing about mine. I so wanted to tell him about some of the strange people I'd met, just to amuse him, but I kept quiet about it all.

He said something that really tickled me. "I don't know who you're working with in there, but they're a peculiar-looking bunch. As I was sitting waiting for you, a group of women came out and none of them had a matching pair of stockings. And then a group of men came out with them and they had the poshest accents I've ever heard in my life. They were talking about somebody called Rupert and how they were going to meet him for drinks in the commander's pad." His description made me laugh. I know he thought BP was the strangest place on earth, but I couldn't say a word to him.

He was only up for one night so we had a meal together and he saw me back to my digs in Newton Longville before walking back to Bletchley. I told him about my experience of walking back in the dark and he roared with laughter and said he thought he'd be OK.

Before he dropped me off, he became very silent and I could tell he wanted to say something but couldn't find *the words. I told him that if had something on his mind he should say it. It was a bombshell. He had been approached by a Baptist college in New Zealand to pursue a PhD through their college with a view to becoming their new principal. The current incumbent would be retiring in the next couple of years and the trustees of the college had learned of his academic and pastoral abilities. Russ had received this approach through his own college principal in Cardiff and was clearly unsure what to do.*

I told him that he must pursue this, but he replied that he wasn't sure how this might affect our relationship and plans for the future. I said that I was sure they approved of marriage in New Zealand! As it was a very initial approach he had told the principal that he would think about it and talk to me. I must say I was very taken with the idea of a new life on the other side of the world.

He was staying in a small guest house in the town and apparently it was so crowded that he had to sleep on a settee in the living room. He didn't mind as it was going to cost him less!

This is a year of rapid expansion at BP. Thousands of new workers are added to the payroll, many of them military personnel. In their midst are a few hundred Americans.

They had a kind of joie de vivre *about them, so extrovert and outgoing. Most of my knowledge of Americans came from films I'd seen. I didn't work with any of them in Hut Six, but I came across them in the canteen. Or rather they came across me! They seemed to make a point of talking to everyone they could and were interested in other people's*

*lives. Maybe they were just plain nosy, but their arrival
in BP was a breath of fresh air. As soon as some of them
realized I could speak Welsh I was inundated with requests
to say all kinds of words and sentences. My name, simple as
it was, was a source of wonder. They'd never heard of Wales
before and when I once told a young man that Welsh was
the oldest language in Great Britain, he remarked, "Oh, I
get it, so England is actually part of Wales." I didn't want to
correct him and I did enjoy the look of consternation on the
faces of my English friends.*

During the spring of 1943, new blocks are opened for the staff
to work in. The huts are no longer adequate to accommodate
the thousands of BP personnel. These new blocks are larger and
allegedly more comfortable, although not in Mair's opinion.

*In all truth, our new block was a bit of a dump. Even
though it was brand new and built for the new workers and
their secret occupations, it was grim and functional. We'd
all become accustomed to the shabby comfort of our huts,
and each one had its own identity. I never really found out
what was going on elsewhere, but Hut Six definitely had
a sense of team spirit. We were all doing the same work;
sharing similar frustrations and confronting impossible
challenges. Mind you, the conditions were deplorable by
today's standards. The heating facilities were present but
impotent to deal with cold winters; I ended up wearing
several layers and still shivered my way through each
shift. Not only was the heating inadequate but there was a
general anxiety about the fumes it circulated; a chemical,
sulphurous kind of smell. Many of us wondered how our*

health would fare, particularly as coughs and respiratory problems proliferated in those small huts during the winter. During the mild and sometimes warm summer months we faced different environmental challenges. These prefabricated huts seemed to store the heat; a problem compounded by the heavy blackout curtains that trapped the heat and blocked out the cool air of evening and night. But it was all homely and familiar to us; these new blocks had less character about them.

The new buildings housed all the hut dwellers and it felt a bit like working in a factory or battery farm. I didn't like the inconvenience of moving; it was disorientating. The old hut, with all its shabbiness, was familiar and settled. I suspect that this feeling was very common during those years. What I experienced was trivial compared to people whose houses were destroyed in London during the bombing and who were rehomed in distant suburbs. It doesn't matter how shiny and bright your new home is when you've lost somewhere that's full of memories and history.

Cheerless, dimly lit, framed by walls of bare mortar, Block D had more in common with a TB sanatorium than an office in wartime. Sundry noticeboards lined the right wall and a curiously bent waste pipe protruded at the end of the room. Suspended fluorescent lights cast an otherworldly haze across the gloom, suggesting an atmosphere of quiet study.

Hundreds of us worked there, although it never felt crowded. Each room's entry had a kind of funnel design, which meant that you only went into your workspace. I think it was meant to discourage people from wandering around and finding out things about other people's work. Even the architecture was designed to keep secrets. The

*building and foundations were solid; it looked like a
hospital.*

Eight of these new capacious blocks are built, housing the 10,000
personnel recruited to work at BP. (Confusingly, the original hut
numbers are transferred to the new block. My mother continues
to refer to this place as Hut Six even though she is now in a new
environment.) But the building and rebuilding could cause
problems – and indeed embarrassment, as Mair discovers during
a late shift.

*I was desperate to go to the toilet, but had been hanging
on because it required walking outside the hut. It was cold
and dark and I really didn't want to go, especially as there
were no lights out there. Eventually I could wait no longer.
So I made my way gingerly around the corner of Hut Six
and into the toilet block, but I couldn't see a thing. And,
of course, I did what you have to do as a woman. As I
was sitting there, I heard somebody shouting out, "Is there
anyone there?" It sounded like Mr Welchman, the head of
Hut Six, but he seemed so close. Then again maybe the cold,
still night was making everything clearer. But the question
was asked again and this time it was definitely nearer. I
looked around me and to my horror I could see that one
of the walls in the hut wasn't there. It had been taken
down, so my back was exposed to the night sky. I hurriedly
rearranged my clothes and shot back to the warmth of
Hut Six. I must have blushed for the rest of the shift. This
was typical in many ways of the constant building and
demolishing work that went on in BP. Huts and walls were
forever being pulled down and constructed, but I never*

*thought that they would demolish one wall of the toilet
block without closing it off or telling us!*

This year also sees the addition of a new kind of machine
invented to speed up the task of code breaking. The German
navy unexpectedly changes its cipher – the code by which they
communicate with each other and their own high command –
and this newly invented piece of technology will be BP's salvation.

In the quaintly named area of London known as Dollis Hill,
Dr Tommy Flowers has been working on a machine called the
Colossus. This former Post Office engineer has worked his way
through the ranks and is completely unlike the other senior
managers in BP in speech and manners. Recruited from the
General Post Office's Dollis Hill base in 1943, Flowers is pivotal in
the development of the Colossus. Often heralded as the prototype
of the modern personal computer, Flowers uses a huge number
of electronic valves to create speed in deciphering ever more
sophisticated German codes. The first version of the Colossus was
delivered in January 1944, using 1,600 valves capable of analyzing
5,000 characters per second. Not only is this a breakthrough in
terms of the war, it is widely accepted that this technology will
change the world.

*Tommy Flowers was different to all the others. He hadn't
been to university and he had a very pronounced East
End accent. He sounded more like someone from the
Covent Garden fruit market than a lecture theatre. He
had obviously worked his way up in the GPO and his
knowledge was crucial to all of us in BP. Mind you, I think
the Oxbridge set did look down on him. Maybe they were
threatened by his success. Those men all came from the*

*same sort of academic background whereas Flowers was
an ordinary working man. This was the only instance I
can remember of class prejudice in BP. It wasn't overt, but
Flowers was definitely treated with less deference, at least to
begin with, than Alan Turing.*

Together with Alan Turing, they create a device which will
transform the Allies' ability to decode enemy intelligence. This is
the world's first totally electronic programmable computer, and
will give BP a huge fillip in its deciphering work. Programmed to
penetrate the Germans' Enigma variations, the Colossus churns
out the rich intelligence known as Ultra that turns the tide of
war in favour of the Allied troops. The Colossus harnesses the
power of several bombe machines and cuts down the time taken
to analyze the settings used.

The mix of new faces and nationalities moving into new BP
also seems to herald an even tighter approach to confidentiality
and security. Posters and memos appear, warning about the
consequences of careless talk. Rumours abound of people who
have been instantly dismissed for talking about their work outside
their huts, but as there is no central gathering point, apart from the
canteen, these incidents rarely grip the minds of the staff. The fear
of being caught speaking about other people's misdemeanours is
also so strong that gossip doesn't spread. But while still working
in Hut Six, Mair witnesses the power of the Official Secrets Act.

*It was lunchtime, sometime towards the end of May, and
a group of us were in the canteen. Mary and Gillian were
especially worked up about something, and in heated
conversation. I couldn't hear what they were talking about,
but I had a feeling it involved a man. Mary had been dating*

one of the officers in Hut Eight who had also taken a bit of a shine to Gillian. Maybe that's how the argument started, but it spilled over into other more immediate and sensitive issues.

Riled by Gillian's cool manner, Mary got into a fevered state and said that her boyfriend had entrusted her with more secrets than Gillian. These included revelations about Hut Eight's success during the Battle of the Atlantic, breaking codes relating to the whereabouts of U-boats and protecting merchant ships. She went on: "And I bet you didn't know that it was Hut Eight that broke the codes in North Africa which led to Rommel's defeat."

By this time everyone around the table was transfixed by this conversation, as were a number of other people. I think we all realized that the girls had crossed over the line and could be in trouble if they carried on. But Gillian wasn't going to stand down so easily, and she too was raising her voice and looking flushed: "Well, that's very interesting, but I bet you didn't know that we probably knew about the bombing of Pearl Harbor before it happened. We could have stopped it, but we didn't because we wanted the Americans to be forced into the war. He also says it's a scandal that Hut Six didn't stop the Blitz because we should have seen it happening."

Everyone froze and went silent. Both girls realized that they had taken this too far and I looked around the crowded canteen to see if anyone was coming to tell them off. After a few moments, Mary looked as though she was going to reply, but I piped up and told them both not to say any more or they would be in serious trouble. They were both, I think, surprised at my intervention and stopped. We all dispersed and made our way back to the hut. Sadly, however, this wasn't the end of it. Mary looked rattled and furious; I thought she was going to hit Gillian at one point.

As soon as we got back into the hut, Mary started again, in a loud whisper: "He told me that Alan Turing is working on a new machine that will revolutionize code breaking. It's nearly ready and the Germans won't know what's hit them when it starts working." Not to be outdone, Gillian replied but in a higher, angrier tone: "And did he tell you that Alan Turing is really strange and probably a homosexual?"

With that, the door was thrown open by one of the managers. She was clutching a file and looked severe. She said that she had overheard their conversation down the corridor and also that she'd received a complaint about them from one of the Americans in the canteen who'd overheard their argument over lunch. She was furious with them and took them to task in front of us all and in the hearing of everyone in the hut.

"I cannot believe what I've just heard, or the gossip you indulged in during lunch. You have signed the Official Secrets Act and agreed to abide by it. This includes any gossip, title-tattle or idle speculation about what happens here in BP. You have said things which should never have been said or repeated and you've disgraced yourselves. You are both graduates and were employed here on the basis of your intelligence and discretion. You have broken that trust and I have no other course of action than to dismiss you from your posts with immediate effect. You will now gather your personal effects and leave."

A sickening sense of shock settled on everyone. Mary and Gillian looked stunned and drained of colour. For a few moments neither of them moved; they were sobbing and one of them seemed to be whimpering and asking for mercy. But it was to no avail, and they started gathering the few things they'd brought in. The supervisor just stood there, impassive and arms folded.

Mary broke the silence and tried to plead with her. "We didn't mean anything by it, and I'm sorry for what I said. I'm so happy here in BP and proud of what we do." But the supervisor wasn't having any of it. She said it was too late and they should have thought of that earlier. Mr Welchman was aware of their poor behaviour and had given the order to dismiss them. Furthermore, if they repeated their allegations outside BP, or indeed spoke about any aspect of their work or the work of their colleagues, the consequences would be a lot worse. "May I remind you that transgressing the Official Secrets Act is punishable by imprisonment. You can count yourselves lucky today that this will not be taken any further." Within minutes they had left the building and BP for good.

I felt ill and frightened. I had never seen or heard anything like this before. There was absolutely no mercy shown, no second chance offered. They had broken the rules and they must pay for it. I tentatively looked round the room and everybody else looked bewildered and anxious. I think we were all very close to tears. This incident came as a hammer blow; we really had to be secret about everything to do with BP or we would lose our jobs and worse. The supervisor who had not moved from her position then addressed the rest of us. Her tone was quieter but stern.

"Ladies, let this incident serve as a warning to you all that we will not tolerate slack behaviour or loose talk. We are handling extremely sensitive information in this hut and in this place; information that would compromise the war effort if it ever got into the hands of our enemies. May I remind you of the binding oath of secrecy you made before coming to work at BP. This oath cannot be broken for at least fifty years, which means that some of you may go to your grave without disclosing these secrets." And with those chilling words her business in our room came to an end and she left. We all just looked at each other, uncertain what to do next.

We had just lost two colleagues in the most dramatic of circumstances and we realized we could all have been implicated. Up to this point I had never seen this kind of summary discipline executed at BP; some people thought it was a bit of a myth, but not after this. There was no court or tribunal; the BP managers had absolute power.

None of us had responded or got involved with the two girls, but we had on previous occasions. After a few minutes, a quiet girl called Susan whispered, "We cannot afford to be stupid about this. We agree now that we will never talk about what's happened in this room today, at least not when we're here together." We all nodded. Somehow or other we went back to our work, but a very dark cloud came and remained over us in Hut Six that day.

That night in our bedroom, Joan and I drank Ovaltine and tried to comfort each other. Up to that point, Hut Six had felt like a large family, but that feeling had been destroyed. Those girls had been incredibly foolish, but they had said nothing that I hadn't heard before at different times. Their crime was getting caught, and the normally equable management had intended us to learn a very brutal lesson. We reminisced about the girls, finished our warming drinks and went to bed.

CHAPTER 16

1941–44 Rank and File

*I didn't know it at the time, but I was surrounded by people
who would go on to shine in various ways later on in their
lives. I got to know some of them in BP, but there were
plenty of people whose appearance on TV or the radio jolted
my earlier memories of them. The poet Vernon Watkins
was among them; I probably remember him because he
was Welsh and we chatted once or twice. People who knew
about poetry spoke very highly of him, but he was very shy.
Another literary figure was Angus Wilson, who went on to
become a famous novelist. He was a flamboyant man; he
used to wear very colourful waistcoats and bow ties. He was
older than me and he seemed to know everyone. He was the
archetypal Oxbridge type; confident, well-connected, with
an impeccable accent. I never spoke to him, but you always
knew when he was near. He was loud, often cracking jokes,
and had a booming laugh.*

*The most famous face I ever saw around BP was
the prime minister, and I did meet him, fleetingly. Only
Winston Churchill knew about BP. We had a direct line to*

the prime minister and we knew what we did was having
a bearing on the decisions he was making. I'm sure there
were others who knew we were there, but I'm absolutely
convinced that they had no idea what was going on.

And Mair is correct in her analysis. Bletchley Park enjoys a tense relationship with many departments of government. Only top-level military commanders are given access to its Ultra messages (the name given to the intelligence gleaned from the Enigma keys after 1941) and, of course, Winston Churchill. Each day he receives a box of the intercepts and the key is kept on his key ring. This Ultra intelligence was thought by many to be the work of undercover spies deep within the German military.

And Prime Minister Churchill forms a very personal connection with BP. Virtually as soon as he takes over the premiership from Chamberlain in 1940, he insists on daily briefings and updates. In September 1941, while Mair is still settling in, and before she has to go home ill, he arrives unannounced in BP during one of her shifts. Her memory of his appearance echoes a belief held by Bletchley residents to this day.

I saw him coming from a hole in the ground. With my own
eyes I saw the prime minister coming out of the earth with
a few officials. I later discovered there was a secret tunnel
that connected Bletchley railway station to BP, allowing
him to visit without any pomp or ceremony. I was so close
to him I could have touched him. I was so surprised to see
him that it took me a few minutes to believe my eyes. He
wasn't as I imagined him. He was shorter and had quite a
bad limp. There was no cigar or hat or gold chain; none of
his distinguishing features. I'd always imagined him to be

full of bluster and noise, but his manner was measured and even quiet. He looked tired and there were rings under his eyes. Seeing him that close, you sensed the constant pressure he was under.

He stopped outside Hut Six and made an impromptu speech. Word had gone out that Mr Churchill was with us and a large crowd had gathered around him. There was some rubble near the hut – there was always building rubble in BP – and Mr Churchill stood on a flat piece of wall that was lying horizontally on the floor. Because he was quite a short man I think he felt he needed some extra height. He didn't speak for long, but what he did say was so encouraging to us all. He thanked us for our hard work and the way our skills were contributing to the war effort and the victory which we were pursuing. With a smile on his face he then used a metaphor which would become very famous. He said that we were his geese that laid his golden eggs and never cackled. He clearly prized our secrecy more than anything else. With that he finished his brief oration and the applause was deafening. We certainly cackled that day.

He then made his way into Hut Six. Our work lives were so regimented normally but on that day, that afternoon, we were given permission to relax. I followed him into our hut and Mr Welchman said a few words. I can't remember what he said, but he was very nervous and struggled to get his words out. At the end, Mr Churchill gave him a large wink as though to say, "Don't worry, you're doing well." He then went around the rest of the hut, asking questions and making conversation.

He came into the machine room where I worked and I was paralyzed with fear and excitement. We all stood behind our desks as he came by. He stopped at my desk and made a few comments about the machine and how difficult it must be to operate. My mind turned to soup; I couldn't think of anything to say. I may even have curtsied out of silent embarrassment. Here I was, being addressed by the most powerful man in the Western world and Adolf Hitler's chief antagonist.

Thankfully Mr Welchman could see I was struggling and explained to him the complexity of the German Enigma and how they changed their code settings each day. He seemed engrossed in the detail and asked lots of questions. In all my years at BP I never understood how these machines worked and how those brilliant men devised a way of cracking the system, but the prime minister wasn't fazed by any of it.

After a while, he left Hut Six and carried on with his tour of BP. On their way out, Mr Welchman touched my arm and told me not to worry, that all of us were feeling nervous with the PM about.

Churchill's effect on BP and its workers extends beyond encouraging the staff, however. During his visit he calls in on Commander Denniston's room, which is opposite the lake and playing field. He is astonished at the sight of a group of suited professionals playing a game of rounders. This he finds both amusing and disturbing and makes further inquiries. He discovers that there are no mass leisure facilities in BP, even though there is clearly a need for staff to exercise and enjoy the open air. This leads Churchill to commission the building of two tennis courts, which to this day apparently are the only ones to have been built by the order of a prime minister. Mair is one of the staff to enjoy them.

I hadn't played tennis for years, not properly since school, but I did have a few games. It was such a novelty, especially as the weather had turned colder and wetter by the time we could use them. But it was fabulous, wrapping up in scarves and hats and coats and banging a ball around. It was such a relief to do something normal and fun after being cooped up for hours on end. Mind you, it wasn't easy getting onto the court in the first place as there was so much interest in taking part. In fact, at one time it was so popular that people were even playing after their evening shifts had finished. I think it was one of those pressure valves we needed to get all that stress out of our system.

The second incident of significance takes the form of a letter. A few days after his 1941 visit, Gordon Welchman and Alan Turing write to the prime minister, gently drawing his attention to the lack of resources which are preventing greater code breaking breakthroughs in BP. Even though an ambitious and costly building project has been agreed to transform BP and employ thousands of new staff – and will go ahead, as we have seen – there is no indication of how or where these new workers will be recruited. And since the existence of BP is a matter of secrecy, even within Whitehall, there is no political leverage to influence the necessary changes. So the letter is written and hand-delivered to the prime minister who eventually reads its contents.

His reply is prompt and decisive and takes the form of a minute to his chief of staff, General Hastings Ismay: "Make sure they have all they want extreme priority and report to me that this has been done." Written across this minute Churchill scrawls the following order: 'Action this day.' It is from this point onwards that resources and people pour into BP.

After leaving Hut Six, the prime minister visits BP's most famous son.

I later heard that he'd paid a visit to Hut Eight, where
Alan Turing, in my opinion the most brilliant of them all
in BP, was inventing all kinds of machines to help break the
Enigma code.

Mair's memories and feelings about Alan Turing are warm. Separated by differences in outlook and background, she remains loyal and defensive of a man whose suicide in 1951 remains a source of national shame. At a time when homosexuality is still a crime, Turing has to endure chemical castration as part of a regime to rid him of this "condition".

He was treated terribly by the government after the war and
by the nation in general. This man was a hero and he died
in awful loneliness. This brilliant man should have been
honoured, not made to feel unwanted.

Mair remembers some of Turing's eccentric behaviour.

He was obsessed with keeping fit. I saw him a few times,
jogging and running. One of my strangest memories is
of him cycling around the grounds wearing a gas mask.
I never discovered why he did it, but I'm sure he had his
reasons. He was a very shy man. I spoke to him a few
times, mostly in the canteen. He was very polite, but
always seemed distracted, as though he was thinking about
something else. I wouldn't say he was a happy man, but
he was always courteous. I think he had a bit of a speech

impediment which probably heightened his loneliness. Some of the girls told me they'd seen him wearing pyjama bottoms in working hours. I never saw that but I could believe it. There were other strange rumours. Some said he chained his tea mug to the radiator in Hut Eight whereas others said he deliberately fixed his bicycle chain so that it would come off at various intervals unless he counted the revolutions. He was every inch an absent-minded professor with his head in the clouds.

Even though the social strata of BP staff in the early years of the war is decidedly middle class and rising, Mair does not feel excluded. This social mixture is greatly enriched from 1942 onwards with the addition of Americans and the presence of more manual labour. But Mair's memory suggests a classless society.

Something I really liked about Gordon Welchman, and this would apply to most of the top brass at BP, was they never talked down to you. You felt that we were all colleagues working together and that we were all equal. Most of us were graduates, but there was no pecking order. I was surrounded by people who'd been to Oxford or Cambridge, but not once did I sense that anyone was pulling rank. There was no old boy network or anything like that.

It was a marvellous atmosphere in many ways because you weren't aware of class or background. We were there to do a job and that's all that mattered. There were one or two annoying people who clearly felt superior to everyone else, but they were a minority. In many ways I'd known a privileged upbringing, but I was still from the Welsh valleys and probably sounded like it. But no one looked down

*on me or patronized me. And I would say there was also
equality between the sexes. There were more women than
men in BP, so the men had to watch their step! Even though
we had to keep so many secrets and work the longest hours,
there was something about that community in BP that I
haven't seen since.*

This was not a viewpoint shared by Russ. Before his death in
2011, he would occasionally remark on the BP people he met
while visiting Mair in Bletchley. He routinely described them as
the Oxbridge bluestocking set, or men in polo neck jumpers who
smoked, swore and spoke of the empire.

After the war is over, and with his political capital rising, Mair
recognizes another BP alumni.

*Roy Jenkins arrived in 1943 and seemed to be involved in
the inner circle with people like Alan Turing. At the time
he was quite shy, and kept to himself. I tried to talk to him
a few times, especially as he came from South Wales, but
he wasn't interested. I was surprised by his meteoric rise in
parliament as there was no sign of particular talent in BP.*

There is more to BP than the rarefied atmospheres of the code
breaking huts. One of the consequences of Churchill's "Action
this day" minute is the influx of new recruits, many of whom are
Wrens. Their role is to operate the growing number of large and
noisy bombe machines now being used. There are so many that
new bases are established for them. A new camp outside Bletchley,
Gayhurst Manor, is opened exclusively for the new female intake,
as is Woburn Abbey, the famous stately home a few miles away.

Joan and I became quite friendly with one of the new Wrens; her name was Heather, I think. She had been seconded from other duties in Dover and was now bewildered to find herself working in this top secret unit that no one seemed to know anything about. She must have come to one of our meetings in 1943. After that she invited us out to her billet in Woburn Abbey, to which we travelled by bus on one of our days off. Before we arrived in the Abbey we drove through a village called Woburn Sands; strange name for a place so far away from the sea. But it was all very pretty and quite different to Bletchley. There were a few hills and woods and not a brickworks to be seen!

Woburn Abbey was vast; quite the largest house I'd ever seen. Like a lot of these grand homes during the war, the owners had moved out and the war had moved in. There were dust sheets everywhere protecting the furniture and paintings, but the dimensions of the rooms were overwhelming. There were women in uniform everywhere and all of them based in BP. There were rumours that it was haunted, but Heather said that everyone was too exhausted at night to notice or care whether there were ghosts about.

Heather took us into the gardens and these were equally spectacular. I don't know if they'd been landscaped by anybody as famous as Capability Brown, but they were immaculate. They showed no sign of war damage at all. Before the war, Heather had studied at Edinburgh University, although her hometown was in the borders. Like so many of us she had studied German, and this had eventually brought her to BP. It was open knowledge that these Wrens would be working on the growing number of *bombe machines that had been built and which needed constant operational power.*

And there were many others in BP, as anonymous then as now whom Mair recalls with fondness.

The ordinary people who worked in BP were so kind. By 1944 there must have been thousands of employees working in the canteen, looking after the grounds, building and repairing all the huts and blocks, not to mention all the administrative staff. Nobody was treated as a servant or valet, but as an adult. There was such a sense of esprit de corps, of working together. I think we all knew we were different and that this experience would be a one-off for all of us. The war gave us that gift. All the differences that normally exist between people came tumbling down and we felt this very keenly in BP.

This was probably the most vivid and egalitarian time of my life. As soon as I started work in BP, I felt on an equal footing with everyone. I know Russ thought it was all based on class and pecking orders, but that wasn't my experience. For the first time I was judged purely on my ability and not my gender. I was paid well and had an independence I have probably not enjoyed since.

CHAPTER 17

1944 D-Day

After the success of the so-called bouncing bombs in the Ruhr Valley in May 1943, there is a new optimism about the war effort. Under the command of Guy Gibson, specially adapted Lancaster bombers are loaded with bombs designed by Barnes Wallis. When discharged at low height, these spherical bombs will effectively spin backwards and skim across water and destroy some of Germany's most important dams in the heart of its industrial area. There is now a perception that the Germans are rattled by the Allies.

In BP, there are further expansions to its code breaking abilities. In addition to breaking the German Enigma keys, the code breakers are also deciphering Japanese keys intercepted by stations in Ceylon and the USA. This has been a feature of its work since 1940, but through 1943 and 1944, this endeavour is boosted by numbers of new recruits from both US and British military personnel, particularly the navy. Up to this point, work on the Japanese version of Enigma has been carried out overseas, particularly in Ceylon. But this now changes with the establishment of a new section in BP. Many new American and British recruits join it.

Sometime late in the spring of 1944, Mair encounters a young man in the canteen whom she knew in Cardiff and hasn't seen since.

I was in the queue behind a man wearing a smart navy uniform. As I was staring mindlessly at the lapels, he turned around and for a moment we were caught in the silence of mutual recognition in a strange environment. "Mair!" he exclaimed. "It's me, Douglas." Of course I knew who it was, and I was overjoyed to see him. We didn't hug, we shook hands; it's what people did in those days.

I hadn't seen Douglas since the spring of 1941 when he was a new undergraduate. The frenzy of the interview in Whitehall followed by finals and then departure to Bletchley had eclipsed more or less everyone and everything else.

Douglas Glyn Davies takes up the story:

After university I joined the Royal Navy as a sub lieutenant. As I had an aptitude for languages it was decided that I should learn Japanese at the University of London's School of Oriental and African Studies. During the war this college had been relocated to Bedford. After completing my studies … I was sent for an interview to the Admiralty in Queen's Gardens in central London. After the interview I was given a few options. I could join a listening station in Columbo, Ceylon or the naval section in somewhere called Bletchley Park. If I took the latter post I would be involved in deciphering Japanese coded messages. I liked the sound of this proposition and was not really minded to move to Ceylon.

Turning round and seeing Mair in BP was overwhelming. She was probably the last person I expected to meet there. But she had been a great friend to me. I was billeted in Bedford and travelled over by bus to BP every day. The work was very difficult as we somehow had to decode these Japanese ciphers. It's a difficult language anyway, but trying to find the real message behind the keys seemed impossible. But we had a fair bit of success.

Douglas, or Uncle Glyn as he was known by our family, recalls one shift where he and the team uncover a vital piece of intelligence: "We learned that a senior cabinet minister was in an aeroplane flying over Japan, heading towards a group of Pacific islands. The plane was successfully shot down and all aboard died."

But Douglas's experience of BP is shorter and less intense than Mair's:

I was there for a year, as the war ended in 1945. Even though the work was hard, our hut didn't work the same shift patterns as the other huts and certainly not like Mair's Hut Six. The last shift finished at midnight so we always got back to our beds. And the food was excellent. I was well fed in the naval base in Bedford and I must say I enjoyed the fare at the BP canteen. Much of my social life revolved around the base in Bedford, but I did attend Joan and Mair's Bible study group in their digs once. I found it very inspiring and a great help at the time.

Mair has very little to do with Glyn in BP. There is something about the BP set-up that draws its workers into present, immediate concerns. The past is a different country.

We didn't really get much opportunity to meet in BP. Apart from that meeting in the canteen, he came to one of our prayer groups, but those gatherings were sporadic. With everyone working different shifts around the clock it was practically impossible to get people together. During my four years in BP, I don't think we held more than five of those meetings.

Douglas was interested to hear of my growing relationship with Russ. He described us as a "power couple". I'm not entirely sure what he meant by that, but I think he was referring to our common Christian convictions and desire to serve the church. He knew that Russ was studying to be a Baptist minister and he probably assumed we would one day get married and express our sense of calling in that way.

But their friendship in BP is overshadowed by events unfolding on the continent as British and Allied troops prepare to conduct a land invasion off the coast of northern France.

In May a number of new restrictions are forced upon staff. All weekend leave is cancelled and a twenty-mile travel ban is imposed. Meals can no longer be consumed in the staff canteen but have to be taken in the different huts. And there is a surge in the number of messages being intercepted and in need of decrypting. The pressure is overwhelming.

We all knew that something was afoot, but we didn't know what that was. There were repeated admonitions to "keep mum" and a greater sense of isolation was experienced. Even though BP now employed about 10,000 people on a small campus, we were discouraged from mixing with each other.

*Strangely enough, though, at the beginning of June
we were told that there would be a Hut Six dance. These
were arranged several times a year and they were a way
of encouraging people to mix socially. I never attended
these; I always felt a bit awkward. At that time, if you
were a committed Christian, going to dances was frowned
upon – and also going to the pictures, but to a lesser extent.
Anyway, the dance went ahead. More or less everything else
had been cancelled and we were all doubling up on shifts
because of extra work, but the dance carried on! What
made it even more incongruous was that we had been told
that Operation Overlord or D-Day was scheduled to take
place sometime towards the end of May and would last
through June.*

*The workload was now greater than ever. None of
us had any idea at the time that we must have been
deciphering the German's plans for that part of northern
Europe. Looking back on it now, our code breaking paved
the way for D-Day; it must have come as a great surprise to
the Germans.*

*We weren't given any detailed information about the
operations being planned, but we were told that this would
be the biggest offensive attack launched by the British and
Allied troops in Europe to date. This explained all the extra
secrecy and it would have been totally natural to have
cancelled the dance. But on 4 June it went ahead, although
Joan and I stayed home for the evening. Even though I
didn't like dancing and the drinking that went with it, I
must admit I felt some regret. I missed my colleagues, and
it would have been nice to be with them as we prepared for
what could be the decisive event of the war.*

Joan and I went into work the following day, not sure what to expect. Could this be the day? It turned out to be a very ordinary shift – if anything, quieter than the previous days and weeks. The only difference was that we were surrounded by people who were clearly suffering the ill effects of too much alcohol the night before!

As it turns out, 5 June is the planned day for the D-Day operation, but poor weather conditions make this impossible. All hopes are now pinned on the next day.

Lunchtime on 6 June, and Mair is near the lake with some of her friends from Hut Six…

It was a beautiful and bright day and we were outside eating lunch. The day was too lovely and warm to sit inside the depressing Nissan huts. Suddenly, and I mean all of a sudden, the sky was filled with aeroplanes. They were flying low, so low you could see their markings clearly. And their roar was deafening. It's hard to say how many I saw that day flying over Bletchley, but there must have been dozens of them; so many, in fact, that the sunshine was blotted out and a long shadow cast over us all. The noise, smell of fumes and the vibrations going through my body all screamed that this was a very important mission. I had never seen such a display of military strength before, and I realized that this must be a very important day.

What Mair is witnessing is one of a series of RAF sorties in support of the army landings. Between 6 and 8 June, 1,246 sorties are flown as part of RAF Fighter Command. Wave upon wave of British and Allied troops are landing on the beaches of Normandy, supported by massive air cover, in Operation Overlord. History later records the impact of the Ultra intelligence produced at BP on the course of D-Day. The German army's movements are anticipated so effectively that they are completely thrown by the Allies' landing. The German military operation knows little of their enemy's intentions, but it seems that the British and Allied troops are now accurately reading Germany's strategies.

The rest of the year is a frenzy of decoding at BP. As the Germans retreat under pressure from the Allied troops so the messages increase. Errors are now cropping up in the normally careful coded scripts, and Hut Six is passing on huge volumes of decrypted messages to Hut Three for translation. Once again the pressure is taking its toll. Hundreds of employees are on sick leave.

Sometime in August I bumped into Dora and Douglas on the same day. On my way past the main house, I caught up with Dora, who was also starting her shift. She looked even worse than the last time I saw her. Her skin was sallow, putty coloured. She didn't want to talk and seemed very distracted and far away. She had a hacking cough and I told her she should report to sickbay for an examination. She replied that she was far too busy and she didn't want to let her colleagues down. With that, she said she had to dash and walked at speed towards Hut Three. I felt very concerned about her. She seemed very low and I could only assume that her mother's condition had deteriorated since our last meeting. This was the last time I saw Dora in BP.

Later on I went for a short walk around the lake just to clear my head. Glyn was sitting on the grass, reading a book. Unlike Dora, he looked well and happy. We

exchanged a few words about people we remembered
form the old days and his working patterns in Hut Seven.
The contrast was extreme. Dora had been here since the
beginning in 1940 and was showing the strain of too many
secrets and too much work. Douglas had only been here a
few months, but his working conditions sounded much nicer
than ours. His shifts were more civilized and his life outside
BP was more collegiate and generally more fun.

Ill health is a frequent occurrence at BP, and has been since Mair arrived. The shift system that rotates over a three-week period is exhausting.

When I started it felt novel and fun, but after a while I felt I
was in a constant dreamy kind of state, especially during the
night shifts. We were living full and often exhausting days
and nights, trying to save the lives of our troops.

As previously mentioned, the hut's construction and fittings are not conducive to health and concentration, at least not in Mair's experience.

We were shoehorned into the hut and it was always full.
Every month new people arrived to fulfil the work that
had to be carried out. When I had started in 1941, the
heating and lighting situation were unbearable. It nearly
always felt dark in the rooms, partly because of the big
blackout curtains and also the way they'd created so many
rooms in a small place. The windows just weren't adequate.
My eyesight was never that great at the best of times, but
trying to squint at unintelligible code in the gloaming made

*everything seem impossible. The lighting was changed
to fluorescent strip lights, but I was no great fan of these
and still retain an antipathy towards them. That kind of
eerie light reminded me of the old gas lamps we had in
Pontycymer when I was a child, making everyone look a
little under the weather and deathly.*

However, the lighting was not the major problem.

*It was nothing compared to the heating. We had these
boilers that were meant to spread warmth but basically
were slowly poisoning us. The fumes that surrounded
us and that we breathed in must have been toxic. It was
summer when I first started work in BP so none of us
noticed it at first, but during the autumn there was no
getting away from it. A lot of people developed chest
conditions, chronic coughing and a general wheeziness. I
used to think of it as the BP rattle. Towards the end of the
year they spent some money improving the conditions, but
it made no great difference. It could be that the stressful
situation we were in leant itself to infections and disease,
but I'm convinced that the high sickness rate at BP was also
caused by poor ventilation.*

After the summer, a couple of Mair's colleagues are taken ill with
respiratory diseases. They return home suddenly, and after a week
news comes through that shakes Mair and the rest of the hut.

*It had been a warm and exhausting summer, and the
combination of nicotine and hacking coughs made it a
deeply uncomfortable place to work. I didn't know the two*

girls particularly well, but we sometimes worked the same shifts. Most of us were struggling with infections, so none of us were surprised to hear that they'd become ill. However, one morning the supervisor announced in a very quiet tone of voice that one of the girls had died of pneumonia. This had been diagnosed after she went home, and it threw us. Pneumonia was highly infectious and incurable at that time. Nevertheless, I'd assumed it only killed old people... and it had taken the life of someone my age.

As the Allied troops drive the Germans back, the shifts in BP are extended and many Hut Six staff work double shifts. Later into autumn and the beginning of winter, Mair begins to feel unwell. She thinks it may be flu or a heavy cold. Such afflictions are common in BP, and more than a month has passed since her colleague's death so these symptoms are unlikely to be related. She decides that rest and sleep is the best thing to do. Unlike her previous experience of serious ill health, at the beginning of her BP career, she is in a settled and happy home and loves Joan's company. She is allowed a few days sick leave and spends that time in bed in Newton Longville. But the feeling of ill health persists; it seems less of a cold and more of a gnawing, aching tiredness. She notices that she is becoming breathless after mild exertion.

But I went back to work. I felt I had to, that I owed it to the other girls and the country. The newspapers were full of the heroism and success of the troops in Europe. It really seemed as though finally the Germans were on the back foot and running away. So I just had to play my part whatever the cost. I suppose I thought that if I ignored my feelings they would just go away.

At the beginning of December we were finally given a day off and the travel restrictions were eased. I was going home for Christmas and couldn't wait to see everyone again. I thought that if I could just get back to Pontycymer and see Dada and Beti I would be as right as rain after a few days. I would be there for less than a week, but I was sure that this would do the trick. I hadn't told anyone how ill I really felt; my head had begun to throb and my chest was aching. But I was convinced it was only tiredness; nothing that a good Christmas couldn't sort out.

A group of us decided to go to Oxford for a spot of Christmas shopping on our day off. We took a train from Bletchley and were there in no time. It was such a beautiful place. People talked about the dreaming spires, and just being there was good for the soul. Everywhere else in Britain had fallen over like skittles against the force of the Blitz, but Oxford was still standing majestically. Not that I was thinking this clearly on that day. The shopfronts were pretty and the girls were laughing and giggling, happy to be away from BP for the day. But I was in a kind of daze. I was drifting along with the others. I bought a few small gifts, but it was as though I wasn't really there.

My body was achingly tired and behind it all was a dull and draining pain. I felt terrible all day and couldn't wait to get back to Bletchley. I tried to keep up a good front, but I'm sure the others noticed that I wasn't right. When we got back to our digs, Joan said that I must go and see the doctor for I was clearly not well. But neither was she. I don't think she was as bad as me, but she was coughing and looked very fatigued. The next day I went to work, but by now I realized there was something wrong with me. I had lost all *my concentration and couldn't sit still. If I tried to focus on my work I would start drifting off to sleep.*

The following day I just couldn't get out of bed; my legs were heavy and the exhaustion had taken hold of me. I was too ill to go to BP and Joan asked the local doctor to come and visit me. He said I should be taken to the sickbay in BP for some tests. I was too ill to go by bus so I was taken by ambulance. I can't remember the trip there or even how I got into the ambulance.

I was taken to the sickbay in a wheelchair and it was the same doctor and nurse whom I'd seen when I caught the flu in New Bradwell. By now I was very dizzy and faint; all I wanted to do was sleep and not wake. They were very insistent that I must try to keep awake, but I was floating in my head and body. A few tests later, the doctor said I should be taken immediately to Aylesbury General Hospital; he suspected pneumonia.

He asked me about my digs and if anyone lived with me. I told him that I shared with Joan Sessions and that the house belonged to a young family. I remember him shaking his head and saying that this wasn't good news. Pneumonia! Even in my weakened state I shivered at the sound of that word.

Although Alexander Fleming discovered the properties of penicillin in 1928, further research was not conducted for another ten years. Even though it is available in 1944, it is not being mass produced, and not available to most patients.

I was rushed to Aylesbury in the same ambulance, but this time its bell was ringing. I was a lot worse than I had imagined. When we arrived I was given some medication and I fell asleep and slept for hours, maybe days. I don't remember the next couple of weeks; I drifted in and out of consciousness. I experienced some delirium as I clearly remember seeing my mother with me in the hospital room. She didn't say anything, but she sat at the foot of my bed looking serene and peaceful. I felt I was loved. I thought I was dying and seeing my mother felt like an invitation to join her. I didn't feel any fear; I didn't feel anything. I could just drift off and not wake up at all. But there was enough fight still left in me. I thought of Dada and Beti, but I especially thought about Russ, about the life we might have together, and somehow I fought my own battle with this terrible sickness.

It was a horrid period – neither asleep nor awake, alive nor dead. One day in a state of exhausted wakefulness I realized I no longer had any sensation in my legs, and couldn't move them.

CHAPTER 18

1945 It Nearly Killed Churchill Too

In 1944 and 1945 the extraordinary BP intelligence machine has gained the upper hand over its Nazi rivals. The Enigma ciphers are being routinely broken and the Colossus is cracking the strategic messages being sent among the German high command. Meanwhile in Aylesbury General Hospital, Mair is now fighting for her life. Pneumonia is an inflammation of the lung caused by bacteria or viruses. It spreads easily in environments where people are herded closely together: schools, battlefields, slum dwellings – and Bletchley Park. By 1945 it is estimated that BP has a sickness rate of 4 per cent; about 400 of its 10,000 staff.

I had heard about numerous people contracting pneumonia while I was there. And sadly I passed it on to Joan who also ended up in Aylesbury hospital before returning home to Oxford. There were so many people packed together in BP that infections just went round and round. The sound of people coughing and clearing their chests in winter was as common as the other eccentric sounds, such as the message

conveyor system or click clack of the Typex machines we
used. Poor ventilation, overwork and cigarette smoke meant
that people's medical health was easily compromised.

But I was in good company. Winston Churchill had
suffered from pneumonia three times in his life and one of
those was during the war. I gather it nearly killed him.

With no remedy available, Mair's immune system is her only defence
against death. Her condition is so serious that the hospital makes
contact with her father to prepare him for her likely death. He
arrives by train and sits with Mair for the next few days and nights.

Dada later told me the doctor looked very grave as he
addressed my father. I had, it seems, come very close to dying.
So close that I had lapsed into a coma for a few days and my
heart rate had become dangerously erratic. They were also
concerned that my lungs had been terminally damaged by
the pneumonia and I wouldn't make it into February.

It is during this period that Russ rushes up to Aylesbury, now aware
that Mair may not have long to live. A relationship paused by the
execution of war may not blossom beyond close fraternal friendship.

Russ came to visit me on his own, a few weeks after I'd been
admitted. He travelled by train to Aylesbury and somehow
managed to find accommodation through a church contact.
It turned out that they were very poor and lived in a
rundown cottage outside the town. Russ had the impression
that the husband had once been a railway worker but ill
health had forced him to stop work. Back then there were
no benefits to help people.

Russ arrived to find that it was a one up one down cottage with very limited furniture; so limited, in fact, that they only possessed two dining chairs and a dining table. They shared their stew with him in the evening, but he had to eat it standing up. And when it came to bedtime, his options were limited. He was told that if he wanted to stay the night he would need to sleep on the dining table. Russ had already noted that it was small. He was nearly 6 ft in height and the table was probably less than 4 ft in length. And it was narrow. But his options were indeed limited. The lino on the floor was torn and dirty, and the only clothes he had brought were the ones he was wearing.

In his normal affable and accommodating way, he assured his hosts he would be fine. Once they had gone upstairs to bed he eyed the table and wondered how he would fare. Another hindrance to a good night's sleep also presented itself; there was no blanket. He felt awkward about summoning his hosts so he decided that he only had one option. He would have to lie down on the table in his suit and coat and hope for the best.

This he did. It was, he said, the most uncomfortable he'd ever been. The table lurched slightly on the uneven floor, adding to the sense of danger and discomfort. Within a short while the temperature in the house dropped. It was heated by a coal fire which went out shortly after the householders made for bed. And since 1945 was proving to be a harsh winter, there was snow lying on the ground, making the air even colder. Eventually the cold air outside seeped into the lowly lodging. There was only one thing for it; Russ made his way over to the coat hooks near the front door and removed his trilby. Lying on the table, fully suited, coated and hatted, he tried to sleep.

The only way he could stay on the table was by drawing up his knees tightly to his chest. It was so cold it generated some warmth for him, but also produced cramp. Thus his night was spent balancing on an uneven table, knees bent and lying very still to avoid sliding onto the hard floor. On the few occasions he managed to go to sleep, he was rudely awakened by muscular spasms. Eventually he gave in and lay on the cold and dirty floor. Within a couple of hours he was awoken by the lady of the house preparing breakfast. Standing up, to his dismay, he saw his coat and suit were coated in a film of dust and grease. To add insult to injury his hat had been flattened. He thanked his hosts, took his leave and searched for a warm café in the town centre where he warmed himself with hot tea and toast.

Poor Russ. By the time he arrived in the hospital he must have looked like a gentleman of the road; the countryside was full of such people in those days, roaming around looking for work or lodging. What the hospital made of Russ that day I'm not sure. Hospitals were very prim and proper places and ruled by matriarchal matrons. The Nightingale ward I was moved to had a long oak table in the middle. It was where the patients ate their meals, but it also dominated the room. Everything was clean; my memories of feeling better and more awake are full of the smell of beeswax.

Russ stayed for the rest of the day and night. He was meant to return to his modest dwelling that evening, but he'd already sent his apologies. Instead he took my hand and sat in silence. I imagine that during the night the curtain would have been drawn around us for privacy. I was unaware of any of this at the time as I was still unwell, but I roared when he later told me of his Aylesbury adventure.

But the crisis passes and Mair's body fights off the infection. Due to several weeks in bed, however, her muscles are greatly weakened. Her legs are physically fine, but she becomes aware of pain in her limbs. She is asked to get out of bed and walk a short distance. But she is unable; she has lost the power to place any weight on her legs, and she stumbles and falls.

It was a terrible moment. I'd been moved from the isolation ward to a Nightingale ward so there must have been about ten beds in there. All eyes were on me as I took my first few steps and went crashing to the floor. I felt so stupid. The doctors were adamant that there was no damage to my legs from the pneumonia but that the muscles had atrophied due to lack of use.

I was told that I would need to learn walk again and someone was assigned to help me. I was given a daily regime of exercises to follow. To begin with I didn't go far from my bed as I had lost my sense of balance. Very gradually I took a few steps and then a few more, until I was able to reach the end of the ward.

At the beginning of February she receives her favourite male visitors once again, but this time they come together.

Dear Russ and Dada came up to see me again; this time I was feeling much better. It was a much happier experience for Russ. Dada had hired a car for a few days and also booked them into a guest house in Aylesbury. He could be so kind. Even though I was on the mend, I still felt very weak. Before coming in to see me, Dada had an appointment with the doctor and nurse to arrange my discharge from

*the hospital and return home, and he took Russ in with
him. This time the news was more positive. The pneumonia
had left my system, and although I was still weak they were
confident that after another two weeks of convalescence I
would be able to return home.*

In March Mair is discharged from hospital, three months after
her admission. A bed has been made for her downstairs, and she
is looked after by Dada and Beti with regular visits from Russ. But
her war is over. Indeed, the Second World War is nearing a loud
and brutal climax. This year has seen the German army driven
back to Berlin by the Allies. Surrounded by so many foes, Adolf
Hitler and his wife commit suicide on 30 April; the former by
gunshot and the latter through taking cyanide.

On 7 May Germany surrenders, and hundreds of thousands
of German soldiers are made prisoners of war. Huge numbers of
Allied prisoners of war, but by no means all of them, are released
across the world and the grim realities of their deprivation made
known. It will be another year before prisoners of war in the Far
East are liberated and their monstrous ill treatment made known.

The 20 concentration camps built by the Germans in addition
to the 165 sub-camps are liberated between July 1944 and May
1945. Here prisoners are forced to work in difficult conditions
and the death rate is exceptionally high. The seven extermination
camps are also liberated, where Jews and others are sent to their
death in purpose-built buildings with gas chambers and their own
crematoria. These death camps are found in Majdanek, Sobibor,
Chelmo, Belzec, Treblinka, Auschwitz-Birkenau and Maly
Trostenets. Over 3.5 million people have been killed in the camps.

The horror of these places is gradually revealed and reported.
Auschwitz II-Birkenau which is taken by the Allies on 27 January

in particular becomes totemic for Nazi barbarism. Soviet soldiers find 3,000 prisoners in the main camp; most of them are close to death. They also discover 380,000 men's suits and 836 women's coats and dresses, along with nearly 8 tons of human hair. The ovens and crematoria have been blown up.

A similar narrative of death emerges in the liberation of Bergen–Belsen on 15 April. British troops discover between 40 to 50 thousand prisoners, mainly Jews, starving to death. Although not originally an extermination camp, Jews and others have been sent here to die, and 14,000 are exposed fatally to the typhoid and TB which is rife.

Many others have been forced to march east to other camps, part of a Nazi "march of death" strategy. In Dachau on 29 April, American troops approach the camp and discover twenty-nine rail cars stuffed with dead and decomposing bodies. In storming the camp they are driven back by SS firepower. Emaciated prisoners then overpower the SS and beat them to death. Over 70,000 prisoners are discovered in Dachau alone. Although widely reported at the time, the full horror is not known until later.

I'd heard rumours of these atrocities, but the eyewitness accounts of these soldiers went beyond anything I could have imagined. And the scale was unimaginable; millions of people killed in these death factories. I thought about all the Jews I'd worked with in the East End and realized why they had come over. I knew things were bad, but not on this scale. Then I started wondering how on earth we had missed this in BP. It really bothered me; we had all that access to information but apparently hadn't been able to stop this catastrophe.

To make matters worse, I couldn't speak to anyone. I just had to bottle up all these feelings and concerns and keep them to myself. But I did feel a sense of guilt.

This pervasive sense of guilt and concern for the Jews stays with Mair for the rest of her life. Her initial exposure to their plight at the Cable Street riots in 1936 forms a profound part of her worldview. She will never visit Israel, or indeed have much contact with Jews, but she carries a pain and a sense of their injustice to this day.

As Mair continues to rest in Pontycymer, Russ's studies continue in Cardiff. These involve frequently leading Sunday services in sundry churches across South Wales. One Sunday in April, he is preaching at a church in a neighbouring valley; only a tantalizing hillside lies between Russ and his future wife. So, after the benediction and dismissing the faithful, he starts his ascent.

It's a bright evening in late spring and, as the light is good, he makes it to the top. But then his simple pilgrimage becomes complicated. He is faced with three paths and no idea which one to take. He takes the middle way, his usual course. After a mile or so on the ridgeway he realizes he is no nearer Pontycymer. Retracing his steps he is back to the junction of three paths. But the sun is setting. Looking to the horizon he offers a desperate prayer for help. Ahead and above he sees a bird hovering over the hillside and decides that this winged messenger is now his only option before complete darkness descends. He moves in the direction of this strange guide, and after a while he is heartened by a descending path. Surely this will take him to his love. The light has gone and he starts stumbling into deep holes. It's a steep decline and he breaks into a trot but the ground is fiercely uneven. To his horror, as his eyes adjust to the darkness, he is surrounded by craters, holes and exposed mineshafts which he has somehow avoided. He remembers that this area was caught in the Blitz. He gingerly proceeds downwards, but slips and keeps going on his backside, feeling the loose ground giving way and fearing that he is about to drop to serious injury or death.

He's rolling, he hears his Sunday suit tearing beneath him, and squeals in pain as a sharp stone punctures his calf. He's in free fall, bumping down until his journey comes to an abrupt halt. The surface has changed; loose but tight. He touches the ground and recognizes it as coal. More than that, there are lights – glaring, bright beams. He has arrived on the uppermost tip of the Ffladau Colliery. In his ripped, exhausted and injured state, he lies back and laughs aloud, thankful for his unusual deliverance. The blackness of the coal adds to the profound darkness of his location, but he doesn't care; he's safe. Greatly relieved and limping, he makes his way through the colliery, into the town and up into Albany Road.

At ten o'clock, some three hours after he commences his journey, he knocks wearily on the door of number 31. Dada is listening to the wireless and about to go to bed. Mair is asleep, back in her bedroom upstairs, and Beti has gone to her room. The silence is disturbed by the knocker and Dada wonders what bad news must surely await him on the other side of the door. Could it be death in the pit? Has one of his elderly sisters been taken ill? He opens the door and is greeted by Russ; bloodied, his suit jacket and trousers hanging off him. "Sorry I'm late, but I've come to see Mair," he says.

Mair comes downstairs and is bewildered by the sight of her dishevelled fiancé. But the atmosphere turns to mirth as he recounts his adventure. As he describes his nightmarish descent down the hillside, Dada adds further horror. Not only are there craters and mineshafts, but the area is also littered with landmines.

It was then I remembered that the Germans had dropped a bomb on the Garw during their Blitz bombings. I had heard and felt the bang, and that night Russ had experienced the damage.

By May, Mair is up and about and feeling much better. She receives a letter from BP informing her that she is being discharged from her duties with immediate effect. Along with gratitude for her services she is reminded that she is still bound by the Official Secrets Act.

It was warm and sunny when the post arrived. After years of war there was a definite lift in people's moods. Nothing had really changed except the end of the war was now virtually taken for granted. Germany's surrender and Hitler's suicide signalled we had come through, and we all felt very relieved and thankful.

I had mixed feelings when I opened the letter. If I'm honest, my first reaction was one of sadness. BP had been my life for four years and had given me a purpose I'd never known before. I felt I had served my country and felt very proud that I had been part of such a brilliant organization. In many ways, of course, this was good news, signalling the end of the war, but I couldn't help thinking about the people to whom I would never say goodbye. We'd worked together so closely but we were in fact strangers to each other. The level of mutual trust and support could not have been higher, but in many respects I knew next to nothing about most of the people there. I hoped that maybe we would all be reunited one day so we could say our farewells.

Five decades will pass before Mair once again enters through BP's gates. By then, many of her colleagues will be dead and their memories wrapped tightly in the mothballs of the Official Secrets Act.

But there was also hope. I was engaged to Russ and couldn't wait for our new life to begin. Becoming a minister's wife and hopefully starting a family gave me great joy. Dada was happy for me, but I know the aunties were not particularly impressed. I think they thought I could have done much better for myself and married someone with money. I didn't care; I was in love and if it meant that we lived in a shoebox at the top of a valley somewhere then I was happy. And Dada kept saying to me that the terraced cottage opposite where we lived was mine and I would inherit it once he died. This meant a great deal to me at the time. I've never been materialistic, but I knew that Russ didn't have a penny to his name and so a nest egg for the future was reassuring.

On 8 May there are celebrations in Trafalgar Square and across Great Britain. Winston Churchill announces: "We may allow ourselves a brief period of rejoicing; but let us not forget for a moment the toil and efforts that lie ahead. Japan with all her treachery and greed, remains unsubdued." And in Albany Road, Pontycymer there is a street party to cheer the end of hostilities.

It was a strange day. I couldn't help feeling that people were trying very hard to be happy but masking a great deal of pain. We had neighbours who had lost men; sons and fathers. There were also a few injured servicemen present. Some people were happy and singing, but I noticed a

number of men who had a very distant look in their eyes;
their minds were far away on some distant battlefield.

As ever, all my aunties and cousins were well
represented. Dada's niece, Edna, and her husband, Will,
had moved just a few doors up from us and they were
lovely. I didn't have to say a great deal to them about BP;
they just seemed to understand that it was top secret and I
had been in the thick of it. My aunties still didn't believe me.
In fact, by now they thought I was deluding myself and were
just very patronizing towards me. I gave up trying to reason
with them, particularly as my outburst against Edward was
still a source of difficulty for Dada. Edward was with us
that day, but thankfully we avoided each other. He seemed
to skulk around the place with a smirk on his face.

Russ joined us later that evening and I could see
that he was feeling awkward. He'd been an unashamed
conscientious objector and I suppose he felt he couldn't
enter into the day as readily as others. And there were so
many servicemen around, maybe he thought there would
be anger expressed against him. Sadly, the only person to
react against his presence was Aunty Lucy. She was always
feisty, even though she was aged. She didn't criticize him
openly, but made some insinuations and jibes about people
who hadn't pulled their weight. She also rambled about
the parable of the Good Samaritan only being remembered
because he had acted positively, whereas the priest and
Levite did nothing and walked by.

Thankfully, as was so often the case with Russ, he kept
his own counsel, said nothing and probably avoided an
almighty family row. I was itching to get a word in; I'd had
enough of the way Aunty Lucy dominated Dada and threw

her weight about. But Russ kept me in check and whispered that I shouldn't say anything.

Before we ate, Dada asked Russ to say grace and it was beautiful. He started his prayer, "Our loving heavenly Father" and went on to thank God that the war was now ending, but also remembered everyone who was grieving and had known loss. He gave thanks for the sacrifice of countless men and women who'd given their lives for others. It was such a moving moment and it diffused all the tension that had seemed to be building.

After the meal is over, Russ tells Mair that he made a big decision.

He informed me that he had declined the offer from New Zealand; he felt that my illness had changed everything. He had to make a decision and he felt that moving across the world would be injurious to my health. He also felt it wouldn't be fair to leave Dada and Beti. I asked him if he was disappointed, but he was surprisingly sanguine about it all. His heart and vocation was in Wales. I must say I felt a tiny bit of disappointment as I thrived on adventure, but I wanted to be with Russ more than anything else. Everything else was secondary.

Despite the surrender of Germany, the Pacific War continues, with Great Britain, the Republic of China and the USA in conflict with Japan. Despite repeated threats by the USA that it will discharge nuclear bombs against the Japanese unless they surrender, no assurances are given. So on 9 August, two atomic bombs are dropped over the cities of Nagasaki and Hiroshima. Over 250,000 people are killed, half of them in one day, and on 15 August Emperor Hirohito announces the surrender of Japan.

Chapter 19

1945-99 Keeping Mum and Coming Out

Although the fog of war lifts after 1945, Mair's secret remains buried and undisturbed. And there are plenty of opportunities for disclosure during the natural rhythms in a year when an anecdote or reference would be apt – Remembrance Day, countless anniversaries of D-Day and Dunkirk. But she is resolutely quiet on the matter of the war and her part in it.

My father, however, has plenty to say on the subject of war. His conscientious objection to it glows brighter as the decades trundle on. Curiously, it is his narrative of the war, or non-narrative that shapes my childhood and adolescent memories. It is his moral refusal to take up arms that influences my own thinking and, I suspect, that of my siblings. He passionately defends the principle of active non-resistance, citing the various sources that have influenced him. These range from the sixth commandment "Thou shalt not kill", to the Sermon on the Mount, taking in Toyohiko Kagawa, Mahatma Gandhi and Dietrich Bonhoeffer. The latter eventually joined the Abwehr (the German Military Intelligence Office) attempt to assassinate Hitler and consequently faced capital punishment.

Far from being a secret, my father's offended conscience forms our own understanding of the war and the heroism of those who refused to kill others in response to divine command rather than obey their temporal masters.

And so we hear repeated accounts of his appearance before a special tribunal in defence of his anti-war position. It's largely academic, since as a minister of religion in training he was exempt from military service. But he was allowed to rehearse his principles before the panel: it was always morally wrong to take up arms and kill another person. War was state-sponsored murder and Christians should refuse to comply. Human life was absolutely sacred and there was no permission to take the life of another, whatever the circumstance. He did, however, work as an air raid warden and also a medical orderly. As mentioned earlier, after the war ended, he discovered that his decision had caused considerable difficulty to his parents, from neighbours who derided their son's stance. I remember him saying once that he might have acted differently had he known this.

These are not regular discussions, but they are not uncommon. My father is persuasive, passionate and principled. My mother is silent. Even though she has a story she says nothing. My father has an ideology; my mother has a history. Relatives die without any understanding of her part in the great drama of the Second World War and this she regrets.

Dada died without really knowing what I did in Hut Six, and I wish I could have told him. Mama died, of course, before war even broke out, but I know she would have been so proud of me. And I would have liked to thank her for giving me the tenacity and steel to stick at it. Those were her qualities and they were her gift to me.

The silence is everywhere. BP's existence is largely unknown and undiscussed. After the war and behind the scenes, Winston Churchill suggests that the place should be demolished and its secrets perish. Thankfully this order is not heeded. The building is used as a teacher training college and then bought by the General Post Office and then British Telecom. The huts, largely unused and unoccupied, are greatly dilapidated.

Mair and Russ marry in 1946 and their first child Elizabeth arrives in 1947, followed by Helen (1948), David (1952), Iwan (1955) and Gethin (1960). My parents settle in the Monmouthshire town of Risca in 1952 and remain there until 1964. Sometime in 1959, my mother bumps into cousin Edward whom she hasn't met properly since the end of the war. It is a bizarre and deeply upsetting encounter.

> *I had the two girls with me and we were walking in the town. I went into the chemist shop and my cousin Edward was there. He didn't live in Risca, but I knew he lived nearby. He went for me straight away. He was rude, accused me of lying about the war and told me that I had never worked for the Foreign Office and he would prove it one day. I was flabbergasted. I didn't know what to say. With that, he brushed past me and the girls and left the shop. I was badly shaken up by this unprovoked attack. I know I'd rowed with Edward during the war, but that was a long time ago. And anyway, I thought we'd made up.*

After twelve years in Risca, the family move to Llanelli, Carmarthenshire, close to my father's roots; deep in the heart of the Welsh language, radical politics and the home of the world famous Scarlets (the name given to Llanelli Rugby Football

Club). Dora Sanderson pays a visit to my parents. It is now 1966 and more than twenty years have passed since these two BP veterans last met. Dora too has known married life, but her years have been marred by tragedy. Within five years of leaving BP, she settles as a civil servant in London and marries a fellow mandarin in the Foreign Office. After two years of marriage a child is born, a boy. By their tenth wedding anniversary, her husband is dying of leukaemia and doesn't live to see their eleventh year together as man and wife. In 1965, aged thirteen, their son is hit by a car as he crosses Clapham High Street. He is dead on arrival at hospital. Sitting in our home in Goring Road in the summer of 1966, Dora is struggling to cope with both events.

It was lovely seeing her after all those years, but she was desperately sad and alone. She talked about her husband and son, but in a very restrained and dignified way. Her eyes were full of tears most of the time she was with us. Dora was going through unbearable suffering and I think she was drawing comfort from seeing old friends. We didn't talk about BP, of course, but we chatted about university and mutual friends from those days. It all seemed such a long time ago; the war had changed our lives and yet we both knew we were bound by an oath not to speak of it.

She was doing very well materially. She was driving a brand new car, virtually unknown in our social circle. Russ had an ancient Hillman Minx into which all seven of us somehow fitted and which broke down on most long journeys. Her clothes were modest but expensive and she sported the most wonderful leather handbag. It looked like crocodile skin to me. What she made of our home I don't know. I was house-proud but we had a lot of damp downstairs, and one of the rooms was unusable because of the condensation. But bless her, she'd lost all real wealth and I didn't begrudge her anything.

By 1970 Dora develops ovarian cancer, the same type that killed her mother, and she is dead within a year.

Douglas Glyn Davies, his wife, Megan, and their sons are regular visitors. Known to us as Uncle Glyn and Auntie Megan, they have settled on the edge of the Vale of Glamorgan where Uncle Glyn is now a teacher. They too suffer tragedy with the sudden death of their oldest son, leaving them with three boys.

There are day trips, holidays and family visits. There is a particularly vivid get-together at our home in Cardiff in 1972, to which we moved two years earlier – vivid for two reasons. To begin with, I remember my mother saying that she and Uncle Glyn had worked together for the Foreign Office in Bletchley Park during the war. It is memorable also because the New Zealand All Blacks are touring Great Britain and today they are taking on the mighty Llanelli Scarlets. It is a weekday and all of us are at home; it is a national holiday, for some reason or other, for schoolchildren in Wales. It's a bruising, titanic clash, and the Scarlets emerge as the winners in a 9–3 victory. It is the day when famously all the pubs in Llanelli run out of beer and the singer Max Boyce sums up the following day's absentee rate from work in his song '9–3' which featured a line that became the title of an album: *We All Had Doctors' Papers*.

But nothing is said about BP; neither then or indeed in any of the numerous encounters between the Davies family and the Russell-Joneses.

However, in the 1970s a trickle of books are published, some authored by BP alumni. Frederick Winterbotham's *The Ultra Secret* is the first to be published in 1974, followed closely by Ronald Lewin's *Ultra Goes to War*. Gordon Welchman's controversial *The Hut Six Story* blows the lid wide open on the BP secret, but due to its poor editing and limited publication the story does not generate the interest it merits. *Ultra Goes to War* is bought by my mother and signed by her in honour of her own contribution to BP. But she does not elaborate to her family. None of us read the book and we are none the wiser.

It is novelist Robert Harris's *Enigma*, published in 1995 and made into a film starring Kate Winslet in 2001 that proves to be a game changer. The director of the film is so disappointed by the ugliness of the Bletchley Park house that another stately home is used as the set. Although containing a few glaring omissions (Alan Turing hardly gets a look-in), the secret is now well and truly out. My mother reads the book and sees the film. She is disappointed.

It was too showy and lacked really important detail. I wanted people to realize how hard we worked and how crushingly dull most of our shifts were. Our work was heroic, but it was also numbing and boring. And by not filming it in the house it just made it into a bit of a fairy tale.

Despite books, documentaries and radio programmes, she continues to keep quiet about the four most crucial years in her life. The appearance of the *Enigma* novel, however, precipitates another disturbing encounter with a cousin whom she hasn't seen for several decades. Since the war, Edward has known success as a chemist and then as a sub-postmaster in Fleur de Lys, a mining village near Ystrad Mynach in the Rhymney Valley. It is 1995. My mother is seventy-seven and Edward is eighty-two.

It was half term and [my daughter] Helen was down from Aberdeen. None of the grandchildren were with us and we decided to go for a walk in Fleur de Lys. Russ had dropped us off before going out on his pastoral visits, and we went over the beautiful viaduct that crosses the valley. After we'd had our walk we decided to have a cup of tea in the village, and that's when it happened. We were passing a post office when all of a sudden this man flew out and seemed to be shouting at me. We kept walking. I didn't recognize him; in all honesty I thought he was drunk.

But he knew my name and he came up close to me. It was very frightening. I mean, he was furious and florid. He said he'd read the Enigma *book and seen the documentaries and there was no way I could have been there. I had been ill for most of the war and malingering for the rest of it. He accused me of lying about working for the Foreign Office; that I hadn't been there and I was a fraud. He said I might have conned others but he knew the truth about me. I had done nothing during the war. He kept on and on at me, saying, "Well, have you got anything to say for yourself?" As calmly as I could, and there was a bit of crowd gathering now, I replied that I had signed the Official Secrets Act and could say nothing. I took Helen by the arm and we walked away, pursued by his shouting.*

To think he was so embittered by my story that he was still angry after all those years! I don't know what had got inside him, but whatever it was had gnawed and eaten away at him for years and years.

Cousin Edward dies in the early years of the new millennium.

*I wish I could have told him the truth before he went. It
grieves me to think that he thought I was making everything
up. For some reason or another, apart from Dada, hardly
any of my Pontycymer family seemed to believe my story.*

Sometime in the early 1970s I become aware that my mother
has her own war story. But it's as enigmatic as the code she was
breaking. As a thirteen-year-old boy in the then dreary provincial
city of Cardiff, I heard my father once again opine about the
futility of war. I ask her a question: "What did you do in the war?"
She answers, "I worked for the Foreign Office in Bletchley Park."
Me: "What did you do there?" Her: "Oh, nothing very interesting,
just office work." Me: "Where is Bletchley Park?" Her: "A large old
house in Buckinghamshire, not far from London."

Towards the end of the 1980s, my mother adds one or two
details to an otherwise minimalistic war story. She occasionally,
and only very sparingly, speaks of the menacing landlord in New
Bradwell or the frightening walk home to Newton Longville
pursed as she thought by an escaped Nazi soldier. But that's it.
No more.

Despite my mother's enigmatic reply when I was thirteen,
I built an elaborate dreamscape around this grand house in
Buckinghamshire. I picture my mother in a leafy paradise
somewhere in the Home Counties. Uninterested in history, my
understanding of the war was drawn largely from my father's
outspoken pacifism, grainy black and white movies, TV series
such as *Dad's Army* and *Colditz* and, of course, fantasies centred
on my mother's mysterious past.

Not talking about it fuelled my fevered adolescent imagination.
With virtually no hard facts, I filled in the gaps using my escapist
longings. The object of these fantasies was never the war but the

place itself. In contrast to the drab, brown sepia of 1970s Cardiff, Bletchley Park seemed elegant and far off, the lanes leafier, the cars bigger, the weather more clement and the schools happier than mine on the outskirts of Pontypridd. I longed for that khaki green far away reality. In other words, it was better than where I was, and the people more civilized.

I remember thinking that Terry and June must live in that part of Buckinghamshire. *Terry and June* was a BBC sitcom, and this couple's lives were chirpy and suburban. They kept a dog, Terry played golf, and they ambled prosperously through life. Somewhere in that cosy and quiet green belt you would find Bletchley Park, I was sure. It belonged there. For a while I harboured an idea of planning a journey of discovery but feared I would never find it. Like all make-believe places, it could not be accessed by conventional means. You probably needed some sort of password or invitation.

Either my mother stopped talking about it or I gave up listening, but by the time I was sixteen this place had vanished from my thoughts. However, a career move from rural south Devon to Milton Keynes in 1998 awakens an interest in both of us. The UK's largest and most affluent new town had grown fat by swallowing up and absorbing sundry villages and small towns, among them Bletchley. By some curious serendipity, my new post is on the second floor of an office block in the middle of all my mother's memories. Despite the concrete blandness connecting its various settlements, the towns themselves are largely unaffected, so central Bletchley in the 1990s is a faded and less glorious version of its 1940s self. (And it was hardly a pretty town back then!)

Many are the short sunny afternoons in early winter when I stare out of my window at work, the sun's glare reflecting on a chrome and glass building next to the railway station, musing on the little I know of my mother's experiences of being in this place, breathing air that she had exhaled, walking the same streets.

Even the minister of the church we attend refers to BP, not in its wartime context but as someone who has worked there under the employ of the General Post Office and then BT. I am stunned to hear that this place of legend has been reduced to training telephone engineers. Even worse is the realization that it is constantly under threat of closure.

One day I notice a poster in the town, advertising an open day in Bletchley Park house. For a few days each year it is being reopened to the public, giving an opportunity for people to learn more of the code breaking triumphs of its wartime workforce. I ask local people a few questions about BP, but most of them know next to nothing about it. I'm told that Churchill visited during the war and there are tales of secret tunnels connecting the railway station to the grounds. Churchill directed that all the evidence pointing to BP's success during the war be destroyed and local rumours still abound that he ordered the torching of BP after the war.

My family and I take advantage of the open day and visit. My first impressions are of a dilapidated and scruffy approach. There seem to be portacabins everywhere and strange collections of military vehicles. Parking is chaotic and a number of what can best be described as 1970s road signs and markings. My initial reaction is of the drabbest jumble sale imaginable. But we buy our tickets and make our way towards the main house; imposing, but not beautiful or elegant. We are taken to the library, a large room on the ground floor. Its decor, furnishings and presumably books are unchanged from the war. Leather upholstered chairs and an oak table face us, arranged in such a way that make it seem as though Commander Denniston and his colleagues have only just left but will soon return. My heart is now thudding. Our tour guide speaks in the present tense. It's 1939 and a curious group of military officers and civil servants clandestinely gather in this house to plan Britain's greatest code breaking operation. This is where my mother's BP story begins.

That night in the spring of 1999, I call my mother and describe our visit to BP. I inform her that there will be another open day in two weeks' time. Her response is immediate: "We're coming up to stay and you can take us there too."

CHAPTER 20

1999 Return of the Native

By now my parents are aged and infirm. My mother is eighty-two and suffered a major stroke two years earlier. My father, eighty-one, is going blind due to haemorrhages behind his eyes as a result of diabetes. Despite their disabilities, both are able to walk and travel. Within a year my mother will suffer serious post-operative complications, contract life-threatening septicaemia and will be confined to a wheelchair. My father's sight will have deteriorated further and he will be completely blind.

But at the end of August 1999, they come and stay with my wife, Clare and I in our new home in central Milton Keynes. They catch a direct train to Oxford and I collect them and take them to their destination. My mother is excited. Her memories come alive as we drive through once familiar places. She remembers Bicester as it was in the war, teeming with soldiers and army vehicles. A few really well-heeled BP types stayed out in Buckingham; as expensive then as it is now. As we enter Milton Keynes and pass signs to Shenley, Shenley Lodge and Shenley Brook End, she is full of half-remembered former colleagues and their lodgings.

But it all looks so different. It is a city of infinite roundabouts, hidden behind trees with a love affair of concrete and cement.

The names remain unchanged but the place is completely altered. A sign to Bletchley is spotted and my mother issues a squeal of delight. "Please can we go there now?" she asks, as though she is a wide-eyed child. My father demurs; he is tired and is sure that the grandchildren (two of whom are in the car and getting restless) don't want to drive around Bletchley. I assure my mother that tomorrow will be a festival of all things Bletchley and we make for the estate of Springfield.

It's an unusually hot bank holiday weekend. America and Europe are engaged in civilized warfare as they contest the Ryder Cup in Brookline, USA, and the Bletchley Park Trust has arranged another open day. Doors open at 9 a.m. and we're already in the car by 8:45 a.m. This is going to be a full day. Before going to BP, my mother wants us to drive around the town of Bletchley. New estates have sprung up all around, but much of it is relatively unchanged. We pass St Mary's parish church, a hardware shop and signs to Fenny Stratford. Newton Longville must be visited, and my mother remembers her night of terrors walking home on her own.

At Bletchley railway station, my mother remarks that it's barely changed from the night she arrived there in 1941. And as we sweep down a leafy lane that leads to BP, she is full of reminiscence. "I remember this road; it's where you, Daddy [my father], met me and remarked on the colourful stockings worn by the girls who worked there." My father chuckles; he can no longer identify people or colour, although is sometimes able to make out certain shapes.

We pay at the main gates and drive to the untidy car park. "There it is," she exclaims, pointing to the main house behind us. "That's Bletchley Park; that's where I went." We park and within a few minutes we're crunching on the gravel path with the house in front of us. "I never thought I'd come back here again. I'd heard they were pulling it down and that was the end of it. I wouldn't have disagreed with them if they had, in some ways; this place was built on secrets and I can understand why Churchill thought no one should gain advantage over the country through discovering how we did it."

As on my first visit, we are ushered to the main house. The hallway is polished and smart; several room run off it, including the one we enter. On our way we pass a small room containing an old-fashioned telephone, desk and typewriter. It's simple, but the sense of the past is overwhelmingly present. The room to which we are led looks like a cross between a library, Victorian drawing room and a ball room. This is where the original pioneers came in 1939 and where people such as Knox and Turing first worked. As soon as the tour guide starts speaking, my mother is transfixed. She barely says anything after this; quietly and intensively assimilating herself to the environment she once knew so well.

Our tour guide is a well-spoken, confident man in his sixties. Dressed in tweed jacket, military tie, corduroy trousers and brogues he is every inch the retired army colonel. One of a battery of volunteers who are designing a new future for BP, he is passionate about his subject. He assumes his hearers know nothing about BP, and there's no reason why they *should* have any depth of knowledge. Not only is the past shrouded in secrecy, communicating its achievements is bedevilled by complexity. "The odds against the code breakers being successful is something like 150 million million to one. Far greater chance of bumping into Lord Lucan or seeing Elvis on the moon," he says. Everyone laughs, but not my mother. She says he's right; it was very complicated.

"Follow me," says our guide and he takes us to the side of the main house, into a courtyard. There must be about fifty people in our group. Looking up, he points to a tower and says that was Station X, a listening post established by the Secret Intelligence Service and later moved a few miles away. To our right he draws attention to a small detached house, referred to as the Cottage. This is the place where the original code breakers began their work. He makes special mention of Alan Turing's contribution; his brilliant academic past, the bombe and later the Colossus. He tells of the eccentric behaviour and then the terrible and lonely death. Even though my parents have known very few homosexuals, they are clearly moved at the thought of this heroic figure dying in such an inglorious and desperate way.

The guide then talks about BP veterans. My already pricked ears are now even more alert. Numbers of veterans have started coming to these open days and yet most of them are reluctant to speak of their past. This reference to the past is lost on my mother; she is hard of hearing at the best of times and particularly when there is a lot of background noise. I can see that our guide is about to move us all to another location and I sidle up to him; this moment needs to be seized.

Others are talking to him, but this is important. "Excuse me, I've come with my mother today and she worked in Hut Six. It would be great if you spoke to her and gained her perspective." With that he draws close to my mother. Although it's a warm day she is dressed in a coat and looks very small.

However, he says nothing and leads the party out of the courtyard and towards a couple of broken down tennis courts. Surrounding the tennis courts are a cluster of equally ravaged huts. They look to me like portacabins from the 1970s; peeling paint, boarded up doors and windows, damaged roofs. One of them is Hut Six. "From the very beginning, these huts were built to accommodate the code breakers, and this hut is probably the most famous. It may not look like much now, but this place was responsible for some of the greatest victories of the Second World War."

He talked about the shift system and the numbers of people who worked in this hut and all the others. He started talking about the Enigma machine used by the Germans to send coded messages to the frontline troops. But more of that later, he said. Then came the moment.

"We have in our midst today a veteran of Bletchley Park, whom I believe worked in Hut Six, the one which we are standing outside now." Realizing that my mother is very hard of hearing, he asks in a loud voice: "Madam, would you like to tell us what you did here in Hut Six?"

My mother's reply is instant and deeply instinctive: "No, I couldn't possibly, I signed the Official Secrets Act and I'm bound under oath. I can't say anything." This small and formidable woman is repeating the mantra she used more than fifty-five years earlier. She cannot and she will not betray her secrets. A wave of laughter passes over the crowd; not an outburst of mockery or insult, but a kind of joy and amazement at my mother's refusal to break her silence. By now there are very few BP secrets left, but my mother is not partaking in this spirit of openness.

"Every time we have a BP veteran here I ask the same question, and every time it's the same answer," says the guide. "It was drummed into them that the Official Secrets Act could not be broken at any cost, and they will not."

We are shown around various other buildings, and see a replica of the Colossus machine that is still being built. By now most of our party is tired and in need of refreshment. One of the huts has been turned into a themed canteen, adopting the atmosphere of a Second World War NAAFI. Tea, biscuits and a Vera Lynn soundtrack sound appealing, but not to my mother. "You go in there if you want to, but Russ and I have more to see."

With that she takes hold of my father's arm and marches him across a large lawn that leads to a series of drab-looking concrete buildings. These are individual museums dedicated to different aspects of the war. Some of them are specific to BP, others are not. It's hot, very bright and my father, dressed inevitably in suit and tie and dark glasses, is paraded across the grass by the most determined woman I've ever known. I look at them as they retreat into one of the outhouses and marvel at their energy and fight.

Clare and I leave the canteen eventually and potter around the various attractions. After a few hours we are reunited with my parents. They are clearly fatigued, but my mother has drunk this well dry. They need rest and food, but my mother has a new and extraordinary tale to tell.

We were in one of those new museums and a couple came up to us. They looked a bit younger than us and I remembered them from the tour party we were in at the start of the day. He was German but had very good English. He said he was very interested in my story as he had worked as an Enigma operator in the war. He had been assigned to serve one of the generals and his days were spent sending coded messages to other troops, directing their movements. They had believed until the end of the war that Enigma was impregnable because of the immense sophistication of the machine. There had been a few occasions when it seemed the Allies had pre-empted their movements, but even then it was believed that these

were as a result of undercover spies working in the German
military. To think that I had probably read one of his
messages and may even have played a part in deciphering
it! He then asked me if I would tell him how we cracked
the Enigma. I must say I was affronted by his cheek and
told him no. I had signed the Official Secrets Act and I was
not going to tell the Germans how we broke their code.
And quite honestly I couldn't have told him anything. I
couldn't remember the way we did it, and I was completely
mystified by it all anyway when I was working here.
Thankfully he smiled at me and said we were all made of
tough stuff back then and knew the meaning of honour.

He then stretched out his hand and said, "On behalf
of my country may I apologize for the harm and evil we
committed during the war. As two former enemies, can
we be reconciled as a sign that the past is now behind us
and we are now friends?" We shook hands. It was very
emotional; I had tears in my eyes and Russ, I think, was
crying behind his dark glasses. It was over.

I drive them back home to Wales that evening and my mother is
unusually quiet, wrapped up in her thoughts and memories. The
car radio is tuned to the Ryder Cup golf coverage; the commentary
is tense, reflecting the genteel hatred that is now simmering. My
mother is unaware of it all. She is back in 1941.

CHAPTER 21

2008 Read All About It

In 2008 my brother-in-law, Alan, reads press accounts of veteran BP workers receiving official government recognition for their work. Unlike military personnel, there have been no medals or honours for them in the intervening years since the war. This recognition comes in the form of an official letter signed by the then prime minister, Gordon Brown.

He writes to the prime minister's office and nothing is heard for several months. Then a letter with an official government postmark is delivered to my parents' flat in Caerphilly. It contains a certificate and citation for my mother's service at BP during the war. A commemorative brooch is also included and she is thrilled.

After all those years of silence, everything was now in the open. If the prime minister could talk about it, I too now had the same liberty.

And talk about it she does. The years, however, have taken their toll. At the age of ninety-one, she has suffered several strokes and experienced a great deal of surgery. She remains lucid and sharp in her observations, but her voice is thin and there are gaps in her memory. But she wants the world to know that she too has a story. Her audience, however, is limited to family members and a few visitors.

It's time that a wider public hear her story. The senior staff and top brass have all had their say, but this will be an account of one of the workers and not the bosses. In October 2009 I write a press release, but only addressed to a personal contact in the Press Association's Cardiff office. He has already expressed interest in the story and I know that their coverage will generate further interest in other media outlets.

By the time the interview and filming is arranged, he has been made redundant and so a young reporter visits. She interviews my mother, takes pictures and shoots a section of video. The following day they release the story online and it's syndicated across the UK. Then the phone calls and requests for interviews begin. BBC Wales in particular show great interest. My mother is local, a Welsh speaker and her story is unusual. TV, radio and online news coverage results, along with a one-off documentary about BP.

My mother's tongue is now fully loosened. No more restraint, caution or hiding in the shadow of the Official Secrets Act. She is interviewed by BBC TV and radio and also in Welsh for S4C's evening news programme, *Newyddion*. Even though she is clearly the star of the show, the producers ask that her family should also be filmed with her. So, in the background is me, my sister Elizabeth and my father, who by now is totally blind.

Here's how her story is reported by the Press Association and used repeatedly by other media organizations:

A 92-year-old woman who interpreted German
intelligence during the Second World War has been
honoured by the Prime Minister Gordon Brown.

Mair Eluned Russell-Jones worked at Bletchley Park, the main site for decrypting ciphers and codes, including those created by the German Enigma machine, for three years [sic] from 1942.

She said she was so nervous about the risk of revealing any secret information she was afraid to fall asleep in case she talked in her sleep.

Welsh-speaking Mrs Russell-Jones, from Caerphilly, South Wales, received The Government Code and Cipher School certificate, signed by the Prime Minister, and a commemorative badge, earlier this month.

While working at Bletchley Park she was stationed in a small, cramped hut with about twenty other women, where she sat in front of a machine and decrypted the German code coming in.

She said: "There were letters in groups of five and we had to try and sort them out, which did not happen very often. We didn't break the code though, the people above us did and there were not that many who could do it.

"We had to translate it from German and eventually it got to whoever it was meant for but none of us understood what we were seeing."

She added: "I remember mostly being bored – it was really, really boring just sitting there watching the letters coming through and trying to sort it out."

My mother has graduated from a priestly hush about BP to an admission that much of her work was really, really boring.

A few days later my mother receives a bundle of letters from schoolchildren in Edinburgh. They are all from the same class in Currie Primary School, where her granddaughter Judith is a teacher. The children have watched the online video coverage and their letters are full of questions. Here's an extract from one of the young correspondents:

I am writing to you because we watched the BBC news clip of you! I thought it must have been a very hard job. Especially since you had to keep your job a secret for that long! The hut you worked in didn't look roomy! I thought you must have been very bored working in the same place all the time.

All the letters, without exception, ask the same question. How did you keep it secret for so long? It is a question that could be asked of every BP veteran, some of whom died without telling anyone of their wartime activities. In a culture where social media platforms are used continually to hang out all manner of dirty laundry, such restraint seems impossible.

We had to keep everything secret because it was drummed into us. It was the law and we had agreed to it. The reason why we kept quiet about it all was probably fear; I was frightened what might happen to me if I broke the law and that fear has been with me most of my life. Years and years after the war had ended I remember thinking that if I broke my confidence the government would come looking for me. The feeling was that powerful. But it was more than fear. I knew that the safety of our troops depended on our silence and as far as I knew some of those activities may well have been going on after the war had ended and I didn't want to be the one responsible for endangering the lives of others.

As a result of her story's exposure, she receives an invitation from the Welsh Government to attend a Recognising Achievement reception on 25 March 2010. This lunchtime awards ceremony is held at the historic Caerphilly Castle and is part of a new awards system to recognize and show appreciation for what people from Wales achieve for themselves and for others. In 2010 the theme for the event is Promoting Tolerance and marks the sixty-fifth anniversary of the end of the Second World War and the liberation of the death camps. First Minister Carwyn Jones presents my mother with a piece of glassware and once again she is thanked for her part in the Second World War.

It was marvellous being part of a group of people who were being honoured for various acts of charity and courage. And to think that the theme was the war and the liberation of the death camps in Germany; among the two most important issues to me. I'm still haunted by what happened to the Jews in those camps and it's so important that everyone realizes that it must never happen again. We cannot allow the same evil to be repeated.

In February 2011, Russ suffers a sudden stroke and dies on 1 March, St David's Day at the age of ninety-two. Due to increasing infirmity, Mair is moved to a residential home nearby where she remains today having celebrated ninety-six years. She is mother to five children, grandmother to fifteen and great-grandmother to three, and a proud veteran of Bletchley Park.

A few years younger, Douglas Glyn Davies and his wife, Megan, continue to live in their home on the edge of the Vale of Glamorgan. They have in their possession several books about BP, one of which contains the famous black and white photograph of

Hut Six with my mother in the background. This page has come away from the spine but a large blue arrow drawn by felt tip points at my mother's head with the name MAIR written above. Joan Sessions died in 2012.

After half a century of mysterious silence, BP is now my mother's main subject of interest. Visitors are quickly apprised of her wartime work and duties, all of which is a source of great pride and satisfaction. The qualities which have characterized her life are also those which were the most apparent in BP.

I had the most wonderful time in BP. From the first time I went into Hut Six I felt special; privileged to be there. There were plenty of things I found difficult and hard at the time, but that's life anyway. To think that I rubbed shoulders with some of the most brilliant men that Britain has ever produced and played a part in cracking the Enigma code is a source of daily amazement. To this day I'm not sure how a girl from a quiet Welsh valley ended up in the centre of the action, but I am so thankful that it happened.

Despite the shift pattern and the exhaustion and disorientation, there was exhilaration to it all. I remember someone saying to me that we were on the intellectual frontline. Our warfare wasn't with bullets or bombs but a constant battle with encrypted codes and phoney messages. Every day was like looking for a needle in a haystack, except that the needle was barely visible and the quantity of hay terrifying. This was my war.

CHRISTMAS 2013 Postscript

On Friday, 28 December, my mother dies after contracting a very sudden chest infection. She has celebrated Christmas Day with many of her children and grandchildren, during which she makes a short speech; she announces that this will probably be her last Christmas.

Mair cooperated fully in the writing of this book and was excited, finally, that her secrets could be told. In the spirit of an oft-repeated BP irony, she has been outlived by the secret she longed to tell. This has been the experience of many BP veterans since the end of the war. I was already familiar with some of the stories related in this book, but only a few. As my mother probed her memory and answered questions, other events and personalities came to light. Throughout it all I have been struck by the immediacy of her experience. Memories buried in post-war rubble have been unearthed with emotion and feeling. Friends long since departed have been recalled with tears; some of them have been dead since the early days of the war. As mentioned in earlier chapters, her determination that the treatment of the Jews should be recorded was constant. She has now carried this sense of responsibility to the grave.

The characteristics which attracted her BP employers to her in 1941 have been played out throughout her long life. Mair was able to keep a secret because she was a deeply loyal person. Before his death, Russ and Mair had celebrated sixty-nine years of marriage.

They had plenty of ups and downs, but they clung together in love and mutual trust. In birthday and anniversary cards, my father referred to Mair as his partner. By this he meant that she was his equal in every respect, and he was right. They shared the same values, the same faith, and she was to him a towering source of strength. Her trust in God fuelled her energy and zeal and a copy of the Bible was never far away. This loyalty to the cause, whatever it might be, was evident to all. She was fearless in defence of her children, although in private she could give an honest assessment of her offspring's and husband's shortcomings!

Keeping a secret for more than half a century must exact a toll on the keeper, but if it did it was not obvious to those nearest to her. It must be said, however, that the last ten years of her life made up for the confidentiality of the previous eighty-six. BP has been her keenest subject, and she was happy to tell any and everyone about her secret life.

Her room in the residential home in which she spent her last two years has become a small shrine to BP. After decades of silence and secrecy, Mair decorated her shelves with every book about BP she could get her hands on. Most of these were given to her by family members who share her pride and satisfaction in the heroic exploits of this silent workforce. Like other BP alumni, she drew particular pleasure from the certificate and brooch awarded to her by the government in recognition of her services.

She relished every piece of information received about BP. This might take the form of a colleague's obituary, or a TV programme. She was especially pleased to learn that a film about Alan Turing was in production and would be released soon. She considered him the brightest of the bright and opined bitterly that the British establishment had treated him with calumny. Hearing of the pending seventieth anniversary celebrations of D-Day and the restoration of Hut Six and the other BP huts gave her a sense of joy and even vindication. It was all out in the open. She also had played her part in the drama of war.

Bibliography

Asa Briggs, *Secret Days: Codebreaking in Bletchley Park*, London: Frontline Books, 2011.

Marion Hill, *Bletchley Park People: Churchill's Geese that Never Cackled*, Stoud: Sutton, 2004.

David Leavitt, *The Man Who Knew Too Much: Alan Turing and the Invention of the Computer*, London: Weidenfeld and Nicolson, 2006.

Ronald Lewin, *Ultra Goes to War: The Secret Story*, United Kingdom: Hutchinson & Co, 1978.

Sinclair Mackay, *The Secret Life of Bletchley Park: The WWII Codebreaking Centre and the Men and Women Who Worked There*, London: Aurum Press, 2010.

Michael Smith, *Station X: The Codebreakers of Bletchley Park*, London: Pan, 2004.

Gordon Welchman, *The Hut Six Story: Breaking the Enigma Codes*, London: Allen Lane, 1982.